Creative
Visualization
for Beginners

D0710823

Richard Webster was born in New Zealand in 1946, where he still resides. He travels widely every year, lecturing and conducting workshops on psychic subjects around the world. He has written many books, mainly on psychic subjects, and also writes monthly magazine columns.

Richard is married with three children. His family is very supportive of his occupation, but his oldest son, after watching his father's career, has decided to become an accountant.

To Write to the Author

If you wish to contact the author or would like more information about this book, please write to the author in care of Llewellyn Worldwide and we will forward your request. Both the author and publisher appreciate hearing from you and learning of your enjoyment of this book and how it has helped you. Llewellyn Worldwide cannot guarantee that every letter written to the author can be answered, but all will be forwarded. Please write to:

Richard Webster
℅ Llewellyn Worldwide
2143 Wooddale Drive, Dept. 0-7387-0807-0
Woodbury, Minnesota 55125-2989, U.S.A.

Please enclose a self-addressed stamped envelope for reply,
or $1.00 to cover costs. If outside U.S.A., enclose
international postal reply coupon.

Many of Llewellyn's authors have websites with additional information and resources.
For more information, please visit our website at
http://www.llewellyn.com

Achieve Your Goals & Make Your Dreams Come True

Creative
Visualization
for Beginners

RICHARD WEBSTER

Llewellyn Publications
Woodbury, Minnesota

First Edition
Second Printing, 2006

Cover image © Eyewire and PhotoDisc
Cover design by Kevin R. Brown
Edited by Rhiannon Ross

Library of Congress Cataloging-in-Publication Data
Webster, Richard, 1946-
    Creative visualization for beginners / Richard Webster.
        p. cm.
    Includes biliographical refrences and index.
    ISBN 13: 978-0-7387-0807-2
    ISBN 10: 0-7387-0807-0
        1. Imagery (Psychology) 2. Visualization 3. Self-actualization (Psychology I. Title
BF367.W43 2006
153.3'2--dc22

Llewellyn Worldwide does not participate in, endorse, or have any authority or responsibility concerning private business transactions between our authors and the public.

All mail addressed to the author is forwarded but the publisher cannot, unless specifically instructed by the author, give out an address or phone number.

Any Internet references contained in this work are current at publication time, but the publisher cannot guarantee that a specific location will continue to be maintained. Please refer to the publisher's website for links to authors' websites and other sources.

Llewellyn Publications
A Division of Llewellyn Worldwide, Ltd.
2143 Wooddale Drive, Dept. 0-7387-0807-0
Woodbury, Minnesota 55125-2989, U.S.A.
www.llewellyn.com
Llewellyn is a registered trademark of Llewellyn Worldwide, Ltd.

Printed in the United States of America

Other Books by Richard Webster

Amulets and Talismans for Beginners

Astral Travel for Beginners

Aura Reading for Beginners

Candle Magic for Beginners

Chinese Numerology

Dowsing for Beginners

Enemy Within

Feng Shui for Beginners

How to Write for the New Age Market

Is Your Pet Psychic?

Miracles

Palm Reading for Beginners

Pendulum Magic for Beginners

Playing Card Divination for Beginners

Practical Guide to Past-Life Memories

Seven Secrets to Success

Soul Mates

Spirit Guides & Angel Guardians

Success Secrets

Write Your Own Magic

Dedication

For the greatest visualizer I know,
My good friend
Graham Little

Contents

Introduction   ix

Chapter One
What is Creative Visualization?   1

Chapter Two
How Does it Work?   17

Chapter Three
The Power of Belief   25

Chapter Four
Desire   37

Chapter Five
Stop Trying So Hard   45

Chapter Six
Dream the Impossible Dream   53

Chapter Seven
Creative Visualization 101   63

Chapter Eight
Affirmations   77

Chapter Nine
Overcoming Personal Problems   93

Chapter Ten
Self-Improvement   109

Contents

Chapter Eleven
Success at Sports   117

Chapter Twelve
Career and Business Success   127

Chapter Thirteen
Visualization and Health   137

Chapter Fourteen
Visualization and Magic   149

Chapter Fifteen
25 Ways to Enhance Your Life with Creative
Visualization   163

Chapter Sixteen
When it Doesn't Work   199

Chapter Seventeen
It's Up To You   207

Suggested Reading   211
Notes   215
Index   221

INTRODUCTION

"A man's life is what his thoughts make of it."
—Marcus Aurelius

Creative visualization is the ability to see with your mind. It is an ability that everyone has, though some people are naturally better at it than others. Every time you daydream you are visualizing. Whenever you think, you create an image in your mind. Here's an example. Think about a friend you had in elementary school. Notice the images that immediately come into your mind as you mentally relive some of the fun times you enjoyed together. Recall a time when you felt proud of yourself for something you had done. Again enjoy the images and feelings that come into your mind.

These images are in your memory and you are recalling them. However, you also constantly create imaginary pictures in your mind about events that have not yet occurred. Imagine two teenage boys going to a party. One boy visualizes himself walking into the room and having no one to talk to. The other visualizes himself walking in confidently, and meeting an attractive girl. Which one do you think will have a better time at the party? Both have visualized a situation in the near future, and their mental pictures will decide what happens. You can virtually guarantee that the first boy will have a miserable time, while the other will have a fabulous evening. Their thoughts become self-fulfilling prophecies.

Have you ever imagined what your life would be like if you could have, do, or be anything you wished? This is making positive use of creative visualization. People might call you a dreamer, but if they do, they have no idea of just how powerful daydreams can be. Woodrow Wilson, the 28th President of the United States, wrote: "We grow great by our dreams. All big men are dreamers. They see things in the soft haze of a spring day or in the red fire of a long winter's evening. Some of us let these great dreams die but others nourish and protect them, nurse them through bad days till they bring them to the sunshine and light which comes always to those who sincerely hope that their dreams will come true." It sounds as if Woodrow Wilson used creative visualization.

Your brain is an incredible instrument that can bring you anything you desire. The twelve billion cells that make up your brain possess unlimited potential. Popular belief says that we use only about ten percent of our brain's capacity. However, it has been estimated that if we had one new thought every second from the moment we were born to the instant we died, we would not run out of space. The potential is limitless.

The incredible power of the human mind was demonstrated to me in a dramatic way when I was sixteen years old. I was working in a bookstore during my summer vacation. One of the other temporary workers was a psychology student who conducted a rather cruel experiment to demonstrate to me that the mind controlled the body. One morning, we were standing by the entrance when one of the other workers arrived.

"Are you feeling okay?" the psychology student asked her. "You're looking a bit pale."

The woman looked surprised. "No, I'm fine," she said. She went to her office and closed the door. An hour or so later, she came out into the store, and the student again asked her if she was well.

"I'm fine," she said, but this time she sounded less sure than she had before. She returned to her office. About thirty minutes later, she reappeared and said that she was going home because she wasn't feeling well.

I felt rather uncomfortable with the experiment, but the psychology student was jubilant. He tapped the side of his head.

"The power of the human mind," he said. "It's incredible."

The woman who went home feeling unwell did so because she had accepted the suggestions that the psychology student had given her. He twice suggested that she wasn't feeling well. Because her mind accepted this, she imagined that she must be ill. Her body then acted on this thought and made her unwell. This demonstrated that her mind was controlling her body.

That was my first introduction to visualization. In that case, the psychology student deliberately implanted a thought. However, we unconsciously implant thoughts all day, every day. Unfortunately, most people think more negative thoughts than positive ones.

A couple of years later, I attended an Outward Bound school. This is a three-week-long adventure program, designed to stretch people to become more aware of their abilities. One of the activities was to cross a river by crawling hand-over-hand along a rope suspended twenty feet above the river. Some of the participants were able to cross the river with ease. Others found it more difficult, and a few refused to even attempt it. Why was this? The reason was fear, caused by thinking about falling into the river. This thought was so powerful that they were prepared to endure the taunts and comments of the people who had done it, rather than attempt it themselves. Their minds were controlling their bodies.

Not long ago, I was talking to an elementary school teacher. She told me about a six-year-old boy in her class who had suddenly lost the use of his legs, and was unable to walk. There was nothing physically wrong with the child. However, he was so intimidated by another child that his mind had made it impossible for him to go outside during recess. The child had not consciously willed this on himself. However, his subconscious mind had made the decision for him, and attempted to resolve the problem by affecting his ability to move.

These are examples of how the mind can affect our physical bodies. However, it also affects every other area of our lives. Think about your life. Are you rich or poor? Do you enjoy excellent health? Do you have good friends? Are you happy? Is your life full of abundance? Strange as it may seem, the life you are leading right now is the result of everything you have thought all the way through life. All of those thoughts determine the decisions you make. And the decisions you make determine your actions. The actions you take determine your level of success in life. Of course if you change your thoughts, you also change your decisions, which changes your actions. It sounds simple, but in reality, very few people are prepared to change.

It is not entirely your fault if you feel trapped or stuck. As you grew up you were exposed to a huge number of outside influences that affected the way you thought about different things. If your parents had a poverty consciousness and were always concerned about a lack of money, the chances are that you will share these feelings.

Our minds work like magnets, attracting to us whatever it is we think about. If you are always thinking about a lack of money, the universe will provide you with poverty. If you believe that the universe is full of abundance and you are entitled to your share of it, guess what happens: Your life will be filled with abundance.

Everyone dreams of winning the lottery or inheriting a fortune from a distant relative. If everyone does this, why are most people struggling from one payday to the next? The problem is that although they are daydreaming about enormous wealth, they are also filling their minds with thoughts and fears about poverty. We all have between fifty and sixty thousand thoughts a day, and most people have no idea what percentage of these thoughts are positive, and what percentage are negative.

Norman Vincent Peale discovered the power of thought in an interesting way. He and a group of friends started an inspirational magazine called *Guideposts*. They overcame early disasters, such as a fire that destroyed the only copy of their subscriber list, but even with 40,000 subscribers the magazine was losing money, and it looked as if it would collapse. Norman Vincent Peale and his colleagues called a meeting to discuss what to do next. They deliberately invited a woman who had previously donated $2,000 to the magazine. However, this time she refused to give any more money and told the group that she would give them something much more valuable—an idea. She said: "What is your present trouble? It is that you *lack* everything. You *lack* money. You *lack* subscribers. You *lack* equipment. You *lack* ideas. You *lack* courage. Why do you *lack* all these requirements? Simply because you are thinking *lack*."

This woman then told the group that they had to "think prosperity, achievement, success . . . The process is to visualize; that is, to see *Guideposts* in terms of successful achievement."[1] She then asked Norman Vincent Peale how many subscribers were necessary to ensure survival of the magazine. He said they needed 100,000. She asked him to visualize that number of subscribers. Norman found this hard to do, but a friend of his claimed to be able to see them, and then Norman saw them also. The group prayed to God, because of the words in Matthew 21:22: "And all things, whatsoever ye shall ask in prayer, believing, ye shall receive." This meeting was the turning point, and the magazine became profitable.

Creative visualization is much more than positive thinking. Positive thinking is an extremely worthwhile exercise, and we should all aim to have as many positive thoughts a day as possible. However, creative visualization goes much further than this. It is a process that allows us to take a specific positive thought and then make whatever it happens to be a reality. Positive thinking is one of the steps toward achieving this.

Creative visualization is a process that enables you to focus your mind on what you desire, rather than on what you wish to avoid. When you do this correctly, your mind starts working to bring to you whatever it is you want. How to do this is the subject of this book.

CHAPTER ONE

WHAT IS CREATIVE VISUALIZATION?

"The mind is everything; what you think, you become."

—BUDDHA

"When I was very young," said Arnold Schwarzenegger, "I visualized myself being and having what it was I wanted. Mentally I never had any doubts about it. The mind is really so incredible. Before I won my first Mr. Universe title, I walked around the tournament like I owned it. The title was already mine. I had won it so many times in my mind that there was no doubt I would win it. Then when I moved on to the movies, the same thing. I visualized myself being a famous actor and earning big money. I could feel and taste success. I just knew it would all happen."[1]

Creative visualization is the art of creating pictures in your mind to obtain whatever it is that you desire. Some people, such as Arnold Schwarzenegger, use it instinctively, but most people need to learn how to do it. It is arguably the most useful skill you could ever master, as it can totally transform your life. You can use creative visualization to change your circumstances, progress in your career, improve your health, eliminate negative habits, and even attract love, money, and any other goal. Amazingly, there is nothing strange or remarkable about this incredible creative power that we all possess. Everyone who has achieved great success in life has used this power consciously or unconsciously.

Walt Disney is an example of someone who believed in creative visualization and used it to create his entertainment empire. He called the process "imagineering." When you visit Disneyland or Disney World you are seeing examples of "the dream that you wish will come true."

Many years ago, I heard a story that I like to think is true. Apparently, years after Disneyland and Disney World were completed, someone said to Mike Vance, the Creative Director of Walt Disney Studios, "Isn't it a shame that Walt Disney didn't live long enough to see this?" Apparently, Mike Vance replied, "But he did see it. That's why it's here." Walt Disney may well have been the world's greatest creative visualizer.

No matter what your present situation may be, you are using your creative mind to attract to you whatever it is you think about all the time. If you think you're unlucky or un-attractive, for instance, your subconscious mind will make this a reality. Most people use this ability unknowingly, and are not aware that they can deliberately use creative visual-ization to transform their lives. It's sad that most people use the incredible potential of creative visualization for nega-tive purposes, when, with just a little effort, they could use it to achieve positive and productive goals.

Years ago, I met a man who told me how unlucky he was. He recounted a sad story of all the terrible things that had happened to him. He looked at me in amazement when I said that I believe we create our own luck in life.

"Do you think I'd deliberately inflict all this pain and suffering on myself?" he demanded.

Of course, he hadn't done it deliberately. He was simply unaware that his negative thoughts had created all the mis-fortune he had experienced.

Fortunately, many people are the complete opposite. They consider themselves fortunate, talented, or blessed in other ways, and as a result, these qualities are manifested in their lives.

You have probably heard the story of the half-filled glass of water. Positive people tend to think that the glass is half-full, while negative people consider it half-empty. Both points of view are correct. All the same, which group of people do you think live happier, richer lives?

I'm sure that many people are born with a predisposition toward positivity or negativity. However, this can be changed. If you tend to look on the gloomy or negative side of every situation, you can use creative visualization to change your approach to life. Even if you have become negative as a result of events that have occurred in the past, you can use creative visualization to turn your life around and become more positive. It is important that you do this. When you think in a negative manner, you act in the same way. Your body language, voice, and general approach will reveal your negativity to others. And, not surprisingly, you will attract more negativity.

Thousands of years ago, Aristotle taught that imagery was an essential part of thought, and that we simply can't think without pictures. He believed that motivation came about when someone either saw (or sensed) something, or imagined it, by creating or remembering the image in his or her mind.[2] Over the centuries, different thinkers, such as Albertus Magnus, St. Thomas Aquinas, and Thomas Hobbes, expressed similar views. However, in the nineteenth and early twentieth centuries, this view came under attack, as people were considered to be nothing more than "conscious automatons." As a result, psychologists virtually ignored visualization until Robert Holt wrote a paper called "Imagery: The Return of the Ostracized" in 1964.[3]

Your thoughts create your reality. By changing your thoughts, and focusing on what you want in your life, you have the power to create the life you have always dreamed about.

You possess a magnificent, creative imagination. Absolutely everything begins in the mind. Every time you think a thought, you are creating energy. If someone calls you a dreamer, you should take it as a compliment, as nothing will happen until after someone has imagined it in his or her mind. Daydreaming is valuable, as it allows you to think about what you most desire in your life.

With creative visualization, you use your imagination to create a clear impression of whatever it is that you desire. Once you have done this, you need to keep feeding this thought with energy and emotion until it becomes a reality. You must constantly focus on the result you desire. You can have anything that you're able to visualize. You can ask for anything at all, and know with absolute certainty that if you apply the correct principles, you can have it.

However, you need to be specific. Asking for a lot of money is not a good idea. Money on its own is not of much use. It's what you can do with the money that is important. Consequently, you should visualize whatever it is you intend to use the money for. Do you want a million-dollar home? Visualize it. Picture it as clearly as you can in your mind. Visualize the number of bedrooms it will have. Notice how well appointed the kitchen and bathrooms are. Visualize the grounds and the views from the windows. Spend as much time as you wish walking through your new home in your mind. It is much easier to visualize your dream home in your imagination than it is to think about piles of money.

Albert Einstein (1879–1955) is best known for his general theory of relativity, but he also devised totally new ways of looking at time, space, and gravity. He used creative visualization techniques throughout his life. He said: "Words or language . . . do not seem to play any role in my mechanism of thought . . . My elements of thought are . . . images."[4]

Einstein was fortunate in attending a school that followed the precepts of the Swiss educator, Johann Pestalozzi (1746–1827). Pestalozzi believed the process of education should encourage the gradual unfolding of a person's innate abilities. Observation and visualization were a major factor in this. In fact, Pestalozzi considered visual thinking to be one of the most powerful features of the mind, and believed that imagery was the start of all knowledge.

Einstein practised this throughout his life. At the age of 16, he used creative visualization to determine that the speed of light was always constant. Einstein visualized a cart that chased a point of light. The existing theory was that when the cart reached the speed of light, it would seem as if neither the cart nor the point of light were moving relative to each other. In Einstein's visualization he clearly saw that if he was sitting on the cart, the point of light constantly moved up and down as it rode the wave of light.

I came across an interesting example of creative visualization in a book called *This is Earl Nightingale*.[5] Earl Nightingale told the story of a man who had become extremely wealthy in the lumber industry. When reporters asked him how he had done it, he told them that he sat every night in a darkened room and meditated, trying to visualize how the lumber industry would be conducted in another ten years. He wrote down any ideas that came to him, and implemented them in his business right away. His evening visualization sessions put him ten years ahead of his competitors, and he made millions of dollars as a result.

Many people use creative visualization to achieve prosperity, but you can use it for almost any purpose. You can visualize a perfect partner, a promotion or new position, spiritual growth, abundant health, and a happy and fulfilling home and family life. You might want to become more confident, or develop a winning personality. You might want to eliminate stress and worry. You might want to progress in your favorite sport.

While working on this book, I came across an interesting example of creative visualization in my daily newspaper. Michael Mayell, a successful entrepreneur, described how he used the technique to find his wife. "I sat down and wrote a list of all the attributes I really needed a partner to have, as well as things that would be a bonus," he said. "Then I visualized it and I affirmed it and I just knew I was going to pull this person into my life."[6] Six months later he met Melanie, who ultimately became his wife.

You cannot use creative visualization to force another person to do something. That affects the natural balance of the universe and creates negative karma. Consequently, you are unable to use creative visualization techniques to force a specific person to fall in love with you. However, you can use these techniques to attract the perfect person into your life.

I have a good friend who had a series of relationship problems. She has an incredible talent for attracting losers, and despite her total lack of success in the past, she continued to think that somehow she could change each new partner. Of course, sooner or later, every relationship ended disastrously. After several bad experiences, she decided to forget men entirely and lead a celibate life. This didn't work, either. She finally learned the techniques of creative visualization, and has now found "Mr. Right." He possesses all the qualities that she visualized, and she finds it hard to understand how she had sent out the wrong message to the universe for so many years.

This is just one example of someone who used creative visualization to attract the right partner. My friend finally managed to send out the qualities she desired, and did not request a specific person by name.

An acquaintance of mine named Brendan wanted to play the oboe. He had inherited an instrument several years earlier, and occasionally thought about having lessons. When he finally decided to do something about it, he couldn't find a teacher. He found teachers of other instruments, but no one was able to suggest someone in his town who could teach him the oboe.

He started visualizing himself having regular lessons with a wonderful teacher. Nothing happened for several weeks. One evening, he and his wife were at the movies when the man sitting next to him appeared to have a heart attack. Brendan helped the man get comfortable and arranged for an ambulance. He sat with the man and his partner in the lobby until the paramedics arrived. About a week later, a small advertisement appeared in the local paper thanking the kind stranger for his help, and asking him to make contact. Brendan phoned the man and was delighted to find that the attack had not been as bad as he had feared. In the course of the conversation, Brendan learned that the man played the oboe, and would be delighted to teach him. The universe had enabled Brendan's visualization to work.

I had a similar experience a couple of years ago. I had been studying the I Ching, but was unhappy with the imprecise interpretations that this great oracle produced. I was on the verge of giving up my studies, when my wife suggested that I visualize myself learning the I Ching from an expert on the subject. A month or so later, I was in a shopping mall and an elderly Chinese man came up to me. He had been to a talk I had given several months previously, and wanted to thank me. I was grateful for his thanks, but his next words stunned me. He asked me if I'd like to learn the I Ching from him. For the last two years I have enjoyed weekly lessons from him. He refuses any payment, but allows me to buy him lunch after each lesson.

A few weeks ago I had a drink with a friend. He told me about the problems he was having with a family who had moved into the house next to his. He told me that the phrase "neighbors from hell" did not even begin to describe the situation. Everything they did upset him, and he was planning to tell them exactly what he thought of them. I asked him if he thought that was a good idea. He shrugged and said that he couldn't think of anything else he could do.

I suggested that he sit down quietly, and visualize himself having a pleasant conversation with the neighbors. He should picture himself discussing his concerns with them in a quiet, friendly, reasonable way. By doing this, he might defuse a potentially dangerous situation, and might even find them to be pleasant, friendly, and agreeable. He agreed to try it, and told me a few days later that it had worked out extremely well. The neighbors were aggressive and angry when he knocked on their door, but soon invited him inside. They had a pleasant conversation, and by the end of it all the problems had been resolved. My friend accused me of putting a magic spell on him. In fact, it was his creative visualization that ensured success. Instead of approaching the neighbors expecting trouble, he knocked on the door anticipating a positive resolution.

This example shows that creative visualization can be used for almost everything. The only limits are those that you create yourself.

There are four essential ingredients to achieve success at creative visualization. Obviously, you need to visualize your goal. You do this by "seeing" it in your mind. The second step is to use mental imagery. This means clothing your desire with as many senses (feel, taste, smell, sound, and emotion) as possible. The third ingredient is to practice. This is a mental rehearsal of everything that is involved in reaching your goal. The fourth ingredient is repetition. The more frequently you visualize your goal, the better.

Let's Get Started Exercise

This first exercise will teach you the basics of relaxation and visualization. Sit or lie down comfortably. I usually use a recliner-type chair or the floor for this. Unless I am doing a creative visualization in bed at night, I seldom lie down on a bed to visualize, as I usually fall asleep during the relaxation stage.

Make yourself as comfortable as possible. Ensure that the room is warm enough, or that you are covered with a blanket. Wear loose-fitting clothes. Temporarily disconnect the phone, so that you will not be disturbed while doing this exercise. Dim the lights, or draw the curtains.

Now you are going to do what is called a progressive relaxation. It is called this because you start with your toes, and then progressively relax different parts of your body until you are completely relaxed.

When you feel comfortable, close your eyes and take three or four slow, deep breaths, holding the breath for a few seconds each time before exhaling. Once you have done this, think about the toes on one of your feet. I always start with my left foot, but it makes no difference which foot you choose to start with. Tell them to relax, and allow a feeling of pleasant relaxation to enter into these toes. If you find it hard to do this, wiggle your toes for a few seconds and then try again.

Once your toes are relaxed, allow the relaxation to drift into your foot. Take as much time as necessary to do this, and then allow the pleasant feeling of relaxation to drift through your ankles and up into your calf muscles. Once these muscles feel relaxed, allow the feeling to drift over your knees and into your thighs.

Once your leg feels completely relaxed, focus on the toes of your other foot and gradually relax that leg, also. Once both legs are relaxed, allow the relaxation to drift into your abdomen and up to your chest. Relax one arm, followed by the hand and fingers. Repeat with the other arm. Now let the relaxation drift into your neck and face, and spread up to the top of your head.

You are now almost totally relaxed. Think about the muscles around your eyes and allow them to relax as much as they possibly can. Finally, mentally scan your body searching for any areas that may not be completely relaxed. Focus on any areas you find until they are completely re-laxed, too.

You are now totally relaxed. It is a wonderful feeling, and one that most people seldom experience while they are awake. It is also extremely beneficial, as it allows every cell in your body to relax. When you are relaxed like this, your brain produces alpha waves and you enter the alpha state. This is a state of heightened awareness and suggestibility.

Relaxation is the first part of this exercise. The second part is to visualize. Think about someone you know extremely well. It might be your partner, a work colleague, or a friend. It makes no difference whom you choose, as long as you know the person well enough to picture him or her in your mind.

You might see this person perfectly in your mind. This means that you are naturally a visual person. Sixty percent of the population use their visual sense more than their other senses. They make use of the other senses, of course, but rely primarily on their visual sense. These people have the ability to see something clearly in their minds. Other people rely more on their sense of hearing, and are called auditory, and still others rely on their feelings. They are called kinesthetic.

If you are naturally auditory or kinesthetic, you may find it hard to "see" someone in your mind. This does not matter. The more times you practice this exercise, the better you will become at it. After all, when you were a very young child and hadn't developed any language skills, you used your visual capabilities all the time. As you had the ability then, you can learn how to use it again. Even if you never get beyond the stage of seeing a vague shape in your mental eye, you can still become an expert at creative visualization.

(If you want to "see" your visualizations, the next experiment will help you develop this ability.)

For this exercise, all that is necessary is to imagine the person in your mind. Some people "see" the other person, and others sense his or her presence. There is no right or wrong way of doing this. The purpose of this visualization is to see how clearly you can imagine the other person in your mind.

Picture your friend as clearly as you can, and think about an incident you can remember that involved him or her. It might be something mundane, such as getting into a car, or eating lunch. It might be something exciting or titillating. Again, it makes no difference what it is. Experiment to see how clearly you can recall this incident in your mind.

The final stage of this visualization is to imagine you and your friend visiting a place that you know, but have not been to with this person. If you and the other person have never gone to the movies together, you might want to imagine the two of you walking into a theatre, buying the tickets, and then going into the cinema. Again, it makes no difference what you decide to do.

Once you have imagined this clearly, take a few slow, deep breaths, stretch, and open your eyes. Congratulations. You have taken a major step toward becoming a successful creative visualizer.

Practice this exercise as often as you can. Just for the fun of it, choose a different person to visualize. Picture other scenarios as well. You might want to visualize the living room of your home when you were a young child. An elderly friend of mine used to enjoy walking down the main street of the town he lived in when he was a child, visualizing all the shops that he passed.

How To "See" More Clearly

It is not necessary to "see" your visualizations. However, you can improve your ability at seeing them, if you desire. Study a painting or a photograph for two or three minutes, and then close your eyes. See if you can recall it in your mind's eye. With practice, you'll be able to recall the picture in detail.

You can also experiment anywhere you happen to be. Close your eyes and see how much you can recall of wherever you happen to be. Don't worry if you find it hard to "see" anything clearly when you first start. Be patient, keep practising, and gradually your skill will improve.

Most people want to skip the early experiments and move directly to a creative visualization. However, you will move ahead more quickly if you spend a reasonable amount of time working on the preliminary exercises first.

In the next chapter we'll look at desire, one of the essential qualities of an effective creative visualization.

CHAPTER TWO

HOW DOES IT WORK?

"Imagination is more important than knowledge."

—ALBERT EINSTEIN

Not long ago, I was on an airplane that had finally taken off after a lengthy delay. I looked at my watch and realized that I would miss my connecting flight. Immediately my heart began beating faster. Thinking about my missed connection created feelings of panic in my physical body, demonstrating that the mind controls the body.

Dr. A. R. Luria, the famous Russian psychologist, proved the reality of this in a different way. He found a man who could affect his pulse by the power of thought. This man showed Dr. Luria that he could start with a normal pulse rate of 70 beats per minute, increase it to 100 beats a minute, and then bring it back to 70. When Dr. Luria asked the man how he did it, the man explained that he visualized himself running after a train that had begun to pull out of the station. He had to reach the last car if he was going to catch the train. Not surprisingly, when he thought about this, his heart rate increased. Dr. Luria asked him how he slowed the heart rate down again. The man said that he simply imagined himself in bed at night, drifting off to sleep.[1] The man's physical body could not tell the difference between the visualization and the reality, and acted accordingly.

Creative visualization works in exactly the same way. Your subconscious mind cannot distinguish between reality and the thoughts and images you create in your imagination. Consequently, whatever you visualize is accepted as truth by your mind, and it will ultimately become real. In the *Journal of Mental Imagery*, David Marks wrote: "Imagined stimuli and perceptual or 'real' stimuli have a qualitatively similar status in our conscious mental life."[2]

Consequently, if you are experiencing limitation in your life, it is solely because you have unconsciously manifested that. Once you accept that you live in an abundant world, you will start manifesting abundance. Once you start visualizing abundance as your reality, it will manifest itself in your life.

Imagined stimuli also affect the physical body. In 1980, Dr. Richard Suinn reported an experiment he had conducted to determine the effects of creative visualization on electric activity in the muscles. An alpine skier was asked to visualize himself performing a downhill run. The electrodes attached to his leg muscles recorded similar electrical patterns to those that would have been recorded if he had actually been skiing.[3]

The brain sees and stores information as pictures or symbols. What is fascinating about this is that the brain processes information from all the senses—sight, sound, taste, smell, and touch—in the same way. No matter how the information is received, it is stored as a picture.

This is why symbols have such a powerful effect upon us. The American flag is a good example. For Americans it conjures up images of patriotism and pride. For people living in other parts of the Western world, the American flag is a symbol of the United States of America, and it immediately brings to mind thoughts as varied as "pursuit of happiness" and apple pie. A flag is a visual symbol, but symbols need not be visual. Hearing a patriotic song on the radio will produce the same response, as the brain automatically turns the sound into mental pictures.

The images we create in our minds affect us enormously. Imagine your reaction if a complete stranger made a rude gesture at you when you were walking down a street. In a fraction of a second, your pleasant walk would change completely. If you were fortunate, you would dismiss it or laugh it off, but many people would think about it for days, weeks, and even months afterwards. This is because of the images that came into your mind as a result of the offensive action.

The pictures we place in our own minds are just as powerful. How does a teenager feel while trying to summon up enough confidence to ask a girl out? Later on in life, he's likely to experience similar negative pictures in his mind when he thinks about asking his boss for a raise.

These negative pictures are so powerful that they can create stress, tension, and even illness. Fortunately, positive pictures, deliberately placed into our minds, create positive feelings and have the power to change our lives for the better. This is one of the many benefits of creative visualization.

Creative visualization is the process of visualizing whatever it is you desire until it becomes a reality. First of all you need to decide on whatever it is you desire. You then have to clearly focus on this desire until it becomes manifested in your life.

You possess an excellent imagination, and like everyone else, you use it to think about all the things you would like to have. Again like everyone else, you have probably noticed that few of these daydreams ever manifest themselves in your everyday life. The reason for this is that you do not desire them badly enough. You want this, but you also want that, and something else looks interesting, too. Your mind becomes confused with all the conflicting messages, and nothing eventuates. They are just daydreams.

Creative visualization is completely different. It works because you focus on your desire, and nurture it with positive energy. It requires a strong desire and a strong belief that whatever it is you are asking for will become a reality. I have heard creative visualization described as "conceive, believe, receive."

Creative visualization is known by a number of names. Creative imagery, guided daydreams, directed imagination, inner guide meditation, mental imagery, and pathworking are some of the other names you may have come across. In magic, the term "willed imagination" means creative visualization.

There are many areas where creative visualization can work. Some people believe that it is a spiritual power, and some divine force enables their desires to become real. Other people feel that the power comes from inside them.

I believe that it is a two-step process. Our minds are like magnets that attract to us whatever it is we most focus upon. Thoughts are the most powerful force in the universe. Just about everything you take for granted in your daily life is the result of someone's thoughts. Your television set, car, computer, and even your toothbrush were all at one time only a thought in someone's head.

Only after someone has had the thought can the thought come into being. Everything begins in the mind. An artist has a conception of what he or she is trying to create before he or she starts painting. A chef has a clear idea of the meal she is going to cook before starting. When you wake up in the morning, you make the decision to get out of bed before you perform the action. Thought precedes the result. To put it another way, the result follows the thought.

Consequently, you need to be extremely careful with what you choose to think about. You have the choice every minute of every day. You can think about success or failure, sickness or health, prosperity or poverty, love or hate. Of course, no one wants to be sick, poor, or unloved. Yet people attract these things to themselves by thinking the wrong thoughts. Whatever you focus your mind upon ultimately becomes a reality. Your mind creates energy. Your thoughts and actions create an energy field that brings to you whatever it is you think about.

Therefore, if you focus your energies on a specific goal, your mind will attract whatever it is you desire to you. To do this you need both belief and desire.

The first step is to use your imagination to decide what you want. The second step is to focus on this thought so that you attract it to you, in exactly the same way that a magnet attracts iron filings. You need to add feeling and emotion to this thought. See it, feel it, taste it, smell it. Picture your desire using as many senses as possible.

I had a conversation recently with someone who told me that he was always thinking about money. Yet he was broke. Surely if what I told him was correct, he'd have plenty of money. Unfortunately, he was thinking about his lack of money, and that is what the universe gave him. This man needed to change his thoughts about money before he could experience abundance.

A man I know quite well is in his late thirties, but has never had a girlfriend. He bores everyone with the sad story of his lack of love. Again, he is reaping what he sows. Unfortunately, he wallows in self-pity, and is not yet prepared to listen to any suggestions that might help him.

Your attitude is vital. Imagine a match between two evenly matched boxers. One has a positive attitude toward the game and is confident that he will win. The other boxer has a negative attitude and hopes that he won't make a fool of himself. Which boxer do you think will win? They are of equal ability, but only one has a positive attitude. That boxer is confident that he will win. Add visualization to this positive attitude, and he would become virtually unbeatable, as he is focused on a successful outcome.

Think of the outcome you desire and focus on that. It is important to clarify your goals to ensure that what you attract is what you want. Once you know what you want, visualize it as often as you can. See yourself accomplishing every step that is necessary to create whatever it is you desire. If you do this conscientiously, it is only a matter of time before it becomes a reality in your life. You can create the life you want by choosing what to think about.

This is a universal law, known as the Law of Manifestation. You can manifest anything you wish. When you clearly visualize your goal, the law comes into effect, and the universal mind enables it to occur. Repeat your visualizations, believing that they will come into being, and allow this universal law to work for you.

CHAPTER THREE

THE POWER OF BELIEF

*"We can believe what we choose.
We are answerable for what we choose to believe."*

—JOHN HENRY NEWMAN

Your beliefs are not the same as your faith. Your beliefs are the result of all the conscious and unconscious information that you have accepted as being true throughout your life. You behave in the way you do because of the beliefs you have created. Unfortunately, these beliefs frequently prevent you from seeing the whole picture, because you view life through a filter created by them. In other words, you see only what you want to see, rather than what may actually be there.

For many years I believed that I was hopeless at languages. This was because my French teacher at high school had told me I was, and I believed him. I saw myself as a "failure" at learning foreign languages. However, about fifteen years ago I discovered that I was able to learn other languages. I travel a great deal, and thought it would be fun to learn some foreign words that I could use in the countries I was visiting. To my delight and surprise, I found it was comparatively easy to learn enough words and phrases in other languages to order meals, ask for directions, and exchange pleasantries. The learning process was stimulating and exciting, and it made the travel so much more enjoyable.

Why was I suddenly able to memorize words in a foreign language, when I had not been able to do so as a child? My beliefs had changed. I had been told that I was hopeless at languages. Consequently, as long as I believed that, I was. As soon as I discovered how enjoyable learning a new language could be, my beliefs changed, and I was no longer "hopeless."

As a result of this, I learned to question my beliefs. Nobody wants to change their beliefs, because it means their whole world changes as a result. Many people refuse to question their beliefs at all, because it is safer to live with erroneous beliefs than it is to face them.

I had problems with foreign languages. However, many people have a much more serious problem: they don't believe they can have whatever it is they want. This is much more serious, as it affects every aspect of these people's lives. These people believe that success, prosperity, and good fortune are simply a matter of luck, and are totally out of their control. The fact of the matter is, of course, that your life is exactly the way it is now because of the choices you have made along the way.

Many of our self-limiting beliefs come from childhood. As small children we accept unquestioningly what is told to us by the important people in our lives, such as parents and teachers. If your mother had said to you when you were nine years old, "You might not be good at math, but you're great at English," you would probably have grown up believing that you were good at English and no good at math. And that belief would have become your reality.

The beliefs of people close to us have a profound effect, too. If, during your childhood, your parents were always saying, "money doesn't grow on trees," "only crooks make money," or "we'll never be rich," it is highly unlikely that you'd be rich today.

Your beliefs control every aspect of your life. This is why it is so important to believe in yourself. When you believe something, your brain acts accordingly. Have you heard that when an aborigine "points the bone" at someone, this person dies? This is an extreme example of belief. The person who has had the bone pointed at him believes that this will cause him to die, and his mind gives up the will to live. Once that happens, it is only a matter of time before he dies.

Another example is the sub-four-minute mile. Before Roger Bannister ran a mile in under four minutes, no one believed it was possible. Once he broke that barrier, hundreds of runners were able to run a mile in less than four minutes. Why is this? Because they believed they could.

Do you believe that you are worthy of all the good things life has to offer? Do you believe that you could earn several times your current income? Do you believe that you are lovable? Your answers to these questions show the power of belief. Henry Ford once said: "Whether you believe you can or can't, you are correct."

Many years ago, a young man I'll call Jason came to me for help in gaining confidence. He was working with a pleasant group of people. Every day, the people he worked with went to the staff cafeteria for lunch. However, Jason never joined them, and remained at his desk where he ate lunch and read the paper. He spent every lunchtime feeling lonely and miserable.

The reason he did not join his colleagues was because he believed he could not walk into the cafeteria. When he had started work at the corporation several months previously, he was told where the cafeteria was. When lunchtime came, he opened the door to walk in. The people already eating their lunches turned to see who was coming in. This traumatized Jason, who went back to his desk and never tried to enter the cafeteria again. In effect, walking through the door into the cafeteria had become an insurmountable obstacle, because Jason believed that he could not do it.

Fortunately, it was a simple matter to help Jason change his beliefs. Once he realized that the door was just a door, and the people on the other side were his colleagues, he was able to walk through it without any difficulty at all. His colleagues were delighted that he had chosen to join them, and Jason wondered why the door had been such an insurmountable problem.

Many people have problems of this sort. They might seem unimportant to other people, but they are crippling to the people who suffer from them. Fortunately, we can use creative visualization to change our built-in negative beliefs.

With positive beliefs in place, you can achieve virtually anything. Every time you see a professional golfer hitting the ball, you are seeing someone with belief in his or her abilities. Before hitting the ball, the golfer imagines doing it perfectly, and visualizes a perfect shot. Imagine how long a professional golfer would last without belief in his or her abilities.

Do you consider yourself a friendly person? If so, other people will think you are also, as you will greet people with a smile on your face and express genuine pleasure at meeting them. Would you act in this way if inwardly you believed that you were shy or unfriendly?

Many years ago I knew a woman who believed that most people were determined to rip her off or take advantage of her. Do you think she greeted the people she met in an open, friendly manner? Of course not. A friendly approach would not be possible until she changed her beliefs.

It is our beliefs that shape our lives. The power of a belief is incredible. Limiting beliefs make it hard for you to create the life you desire. The good news is that it is possible to change your beliefs.

Your beliefs gradually develop as you go through life as a result of the experiences you undergo. Good experiences help you create and reinforce positive beliefs. Negative experiences do the opposite. As your beliefs have such an incredible effect upon your life, it is amazing that so few people make any attempt to change them.

Fortunately, it is not hard to do this. You become what you focus on. If you constantly dwell on difficult experiences from your past, you will gradually turn into a negative person. However, once you become aware of how negative you are, and begin filling your mind with positive thoughts and attitudes, over a period of time your entire life will improve.

Here is another example of someone who believed the powers of the universe would help her attain her goals. Simone bought an old house in a fashionable part of the city she lived in, at a time when real estate prices had reached historic highs. Her intention was to move into it with her new partner. Unfortunately, the relationship broke up before they moved in, and Simone was left with a house that was far too large for one person.

She was a student of creative visualization. She visualized a perfect tenant in her mind, someone who would love the house as much as she did, and would look after it and pay the rent on time. Even though there was a surplus of rental properties on the market, Simone found the ideal tenant in a matter of days. She believed that she would find this person, and the universe provided her with the perfect tenant.

Another acquaintance of mine made a bad mistake when he chose a new sales manager for his business. Over the next three months, all the sales staff left, taking their knowledge and experience with them. After creating chaos in the business, the sales manager quit, too. To the amazement of everyone who knew him, Robert did not panic. Instead he chose to regard the situation as a challenge.

In his regular creative visualization sessions, Robert visualized the perfect sales person. One by one, sometimes in unexpected ways, he built up his sales team again, and his corporation is now doing better than ever.

I asked him if he had ever doubted that the visualizations would work.

"Not for a moment," he told me. "I knew they would work. They've always worked in the past, so I believed they would this time."

Fred Smith, the founder of FedEx, believed in the possibility of an overnight delivery service nationwide. While he was an undergraduate student at Yale University, he wrote a term paper which outlined his vision. The paper received an average grade, and his professor wrote: "The proposal is interesting and well-formed, but in order to earn better than a C, the idea must be feasible."[1] However, Fred Smith believed in his vision, and made it happen.

To become the person you want to be, it is vital that you believe in yourself, and act on that belief. Many people rely on family, friends, and colleagues to give them what they want, rather than taking the initiative and manifesting it themselves. When you rely on others, you effectively hand your personal power to them. Do not give up your hopes, dreams, and ambitions because other people doubt you, or hold you back in other ways. Do you think Christopher Columbus would have crossed the Atlantic Ocean without belief in himself and his capabilities?

The power of belief is limitless. Anything you mentally accept and believe to be true will ultimately occur. Consequently, you should believe in good fortune, love, the goodness of humanity, and especially yourself. One of my favorite quotes from the Bible is: "Ask, and it shall be given you; seek and you shall find; knock, and it shall be opened unto you" (Matt. 7:7). Jesus said: "All things are possible to him that believeth" (Mark 9:23). Believe in yourself and ask for whatever it is you want.

The Body Test

This exercise is an experiment in belief. Before you start, think about a few things you would like to do, be, or have, in the next twelve months. These ideas can relate to any area of your life that you wish. You might desire a pay raise, a vacation on a cruise ship, or a new fitness regime. Once you have a few possibilities in mind, decide which of these goals is the most important to you.

Sit down quietly and go through the relaxation exercise that was described in the previous chapter. Once you feel completely relaxed, start thinking about your most important goal. In your mind, picture yourself accomplishing this goal. Once you have done this, become aware of your physical body, relaxed and totally at ease. Ask your body if achieving this goal would be good for you. Pause to see if your body reacts in any way. You might feel a slight tightening of the muscles in the area of your solar plexus. You might notice your heart beating a little faster. You may notice nothing at all.

Take a few deep breaths and allow your body to become completely relaxed again. Ask your body if your personal beliefs allow you to achieve this goal. Again pause and notice what happens. Repeat this a few times, asking yourself if you are prepared to pay the price for achieving this goal, if you will be happier once you have achieved it, and if your life would improve in any way once you have achieved your goal. Finally, ask yourself if you honestly believe that you can achieve this goal.

Think about your goal again for a minute or two, and then slowly count to five and open your eyes. Before you return to your day, think about the messages your body may have sent you. If you remained calm and totally relaxed throughout, your personal beliefs will not stand in the way of you achieving this goal. However, if your body reacted in some way, you will need to put some work into your beliefs and then go through this exercise again. It is impossible for you to achieve any goal if you do not believe that you can accomplish it. Proverbs 23:7 puts it this way: "As a man thinketh in his heart, so is he."

Naturally, you can repeat this exercise as often as you wish, to test anything that you would like to have manifested in your life.

How to Change Erroneous Beliefs

This is an exercise you can do whenever you find yourself having problems in any area of your life. All you need do is write down all the beliefs you have concerning whatever it happens to be. If you are experiencing relationship problems, write down everything you can think of that relates to your beliefs in this area. If you are having health problems, write down your beliefs about health. Do the same thing if you are experiencing financial problems.

Do not pause to evaluate or censor anything you write. No one needs to see what you have written. You will be amazed at what comes out of your subconscious mind with this exercise.

Once you have written down everything that comes to you regarding this area of your life, evaluate your beliefs carefully. See how many of them you can change around to create new beliefs. If, for instance, you have a belief that it's hard to make friends, rewrite it so that it reads: "I find it easy to make friends." Use this new saying as an affirmation (see Chapter Eight) until it becomes a natural part of your life.

Many years ago, someone came to me for a palm reading as his typesetting business was going downhill. It was in the early 1980s when PCs were dramatically affecting the work of traditional typesetters. He had come to believe that there were no opportunities left for typesetters, and that he might as well give up. He had other limiting beliefs as well. He believed that you had to work hard for everything, that something would always go wrong, and that it didn't matter what he did, because he would never get ahead. I had him write all of these beliefs down, and then rewrite them in the way he would like his life to be. After several minutes, he produced the following list:

- There are plenty of opportunities for typesetters.
- I achieve my goals with great ease.
- Matters always turn out right for me.
- I progress easily.
- I achieve all of my goals.
- I deserve to be successful.
- I like and respect myself.

He was surprised when he read this list, and expressed doubt that he could achieve any of them. I suggested that he work on one or two at a time, and over a period of months, he eliminated his form of destructive beliefs and replaced them with the new positive beliefs that he had written down. Today, more than twenty years later, his business is still thriving and he is extremely successful.

In the next chapter we will look at the other essential quality necessary for using creative visualization effectively: desire.

CHAPTER FOUR

DESIRE

"Desire: the starting point of all achievement."

—NAPOLEON HILL

Desire is an essential part of creative visualization. Nothing can stop the progress of someone with a sufficiently strong desire. There is no point in using creative visualization for some idle whim. Passing fancies are unlikely to be things that you want or need, anyway. However, when something you greatly desire is involved, you'll be prepared to focus on it until it becomes a reality in your life.

Many years ago, I went to a car show with a friend. We had a wonderful time looking at all the beautiful, new cars. I remember my friend spending several minutes examining a Porsche.

"It would be nice to own a car like that," he told me.

Do you think he is the proud owner of a Porsche today? "It would be nice" is a vague, wistful, slightly longing remark. If he had said, "I want it," it is highly likely that he would be driving his very own Porsche today. "I want it" reflects a desire.

You are probably familiar with Jesus's words: "Ask and it shall be given you" (Matt. 7:7, Luke 11:9). That is an example of desire in action. Jesus tells you to ask God to give you whatever it is you desire. This quote also demonstrates the abundance of the universe. There is more than enough for everyone. You can desire as much as you want. There is no mention of entitlement, either. Anyone can ask, and they will receive.

Wanting something is not enough. Hoping and wishing do not ensure success. You need passion. You must desire it with every fiber of your being. By doing this, you harness the energies of the universe to bring your desire to you.

It is a simple matter to determine the depth of your desire. Sometimes it is obvious. If you have always dreamed of being a movie star and are determined that nothing is going to get in the way of your dream, you possess a strong desire. However, it is not always, or even usually, as easy as this. If you are thinking of moving, for instance, you need to determine your level of desire. Moving to a new house because it seems like a good idea is not a desire. It's a passing fancy, and you may or may not eventually do it. However, if you want to move for an important reason, such as to be closer to a school, or because you need more room so that relatives can come and stay, you have a good reason to move. This means you should visualize your new home. It is a good idea to question yourself whenever you think of visualizing something. Ask yourself why you really want it. Question yourself closely. If you can provide yourself with good answers, the chances are you will have enough desire to successfully visualize whatever it happens to be.

When I was a child I wanted a bicycle. I constantly thought of the independence, exploration, and freedom that having a bike of my own would bring. Several of my friends already had bikes, which meant they were able to ride to and from school. I hated the sound of their bells as they rode past me on the way to school in the mornings.

My parents said that if I did well in the school exams they would buy me a bike for Christmas. This motivated me for a while, but after a week or two, I returned to my old habits.

One morning, several weeks before the Christmas break, a friend arrived at school in a state of great excitement. His older brother, and a group of friends, had visited a factory and asked for a guided tour. Not only had they been given a tour, they had been given several samples of the company's products at the end. My friends and I immediately started thinking of the places we could visit, and all the free samples we would receive. The first place we decided to visit was an ice cream factory. The only problem was that I was the only one without a bicycle. As the places we intended to visit were in different parts of the city, I had to do well enough in the exams to earn the bicycle.

That was the incentive I needed. I constantly thought of the bicycle I was going to receive, and of all the free samples of ice creams and toys that we'd be given at the factories we visited. In my mind, I could see myself riding the brand-new bicycle, and could even taste the ice cream. I began studying with renewed vigour, and did better than ever before in the school exams.

On Christmas Eve, my father took me to the local bicycle store to choose a bike, which I proudly rode home. During the following year, my friends and I visited many factories, and received many free samples, but the best of the lot was the ice cream we were given at the first factory we chose to visit.

That is the first instance I can recall in which I used creative visualization. Of course, I had no idea that that was what I was doing. All I knew was that I desired a bicycle so much that I was prepared to do anything, even study, to achieve my goal.

I wanted a bike, and when I was promised one for Christmas if I did better in school, I worked hard for a while, but then gave up. It was only when desire was added to the picture that I was prepared to make the sustained effort necessary to achieve my goal.

When someone genuinely desires something, they are usually close to achieving it. Any obstacles will be overcome, no matter how challenging they may be, as this person possesses the necessary determination, tenacity, and will to achieve the goal. The desire for success is one of the most powerful forces in the world.

You need to constantly nurture and intensify your desires, as they have the power to take you to heights you wouldn't otherwise dream of reaching. People with strong desires are able to achieve apparently impossible goals. People with weak desires give up easily and seldom realize their full potential.

Vince Lombardi, the famous football coach, is credited with saying, "Winning isn't everything, but *wanting* to win is." A good athlete has a desire to succeed that is so strong and so powerful that nothing will stop him or her from winning.

A strong desire, such as winning a particular game, has purpose behind it. It is purpose that makes everything in life worthwhile. Denis Waitley and Reni L. Witt wrote: "Without purpose, work and life become meaningless exercises in futility . . . Without a sense of purpose, work becomes a prison." [1]

When I was growing up, I came to know a man who walked past our house every couple of weeks, dragging a lawn mower behind him. I used to feel sorry for him, until someone told us that he was a millionaire. He was taking the mower to mow the lawns of properties he owned. What made this story even more remarkable for me was that he spoke very little English. He had arrived as a refugee, without family or possessions. Yet in a handful of years he had become wealthy. When I asked him about it, he placed his hands on his heart and told me he had passion. "With passion you can achieve anything," he told me. I wasn't entirely sure what he meant at the time, but I remember his words as he spoke them with passion. I believed him.

Here is an interesting experiment if you are not sure what you desire. Sit down quietly and think about something that you thoroughly enjoy doing. It makes no difference if this is connected with your work, home life, or hobbies. Once you have something in mind, see how far you can take the idea without it becoming totally impossible. You might, for instance, enjoy creating mosaics. While thinking about this hobby, you might think of teaching the craft of mosaics to others. You might then think that perhaps you could make a living out of creating beautiful mosaics to sell. This thought might encourage you to think that you could create large mosaic sculptures for people to have in their gardens. If this is your hobby, you need to keep on brainstorming in this way until you reach a point that appears totally impossible. Once you reach the point that seems impossible, think about it for a minute or two, and see if the idea is within the bounds of possibility after all. If it is, that will become your goal. If it still seems impossible, go back one step to the idea that occurred to you immediately before the final one, and see if it seems possible. You are looking for a goal, inside a field that you love, but a goal that excites and scares you at the same time. This can be your magnificent obsession.

You might think this is fine if you have a creative hobby, but what if you have no special skills? Let's take something as mundane as enjoying watching soap operas on TV. If you brainstorm that, you might come up with becoming a reviewer of TV programs. Maybe you could write a weekly article on your favorite programs. Take it a step further. Maybe you could set up a fan club for other people who enjoy your favorite program. Maybe you could get a job in television. Hey, maybe you could become a TV producer!

A friend of mine is living the life of his dreams as a direct result of doing this exercise. He was a schoolteacher who enjoyed performing magic tricks as a hobby. His first thought was that maybe he could do children's magic shows on the weekends and make a bit of extra money. This led him to thinking he could become a full-time magician. Ultimately, he found the idea that excited and terrified him: he would perform his magic act on cruise ships. Nowadays, he sends me postcards from all around the world.

Once you know what you want, and have purpose behind it, you have effectively set yourself a goal. Goals require action. Goals are doing activities. Before we start doing, though, we must first "be."

CHAPTER FIVE

STOP TRYING SO HARD

*"Without this playing with fantasy no creative work
has ever yet come to birth. The debt we owe to the play
of imagination is incalculable."*

—CARL JUNG

There is an old saying that the only people who don't suffer from stress are in graveyards. Of course, there is good stress and bad stress. We need a certain degree of positive stress to accomplish anything, but negative stress is debilitating, and can even kill people who suffer from it.

There are more stresses on people today than ever before. Financial pressures, relationship problems, gridlock traffic, and the constant drive to get ahead in one's career all create negative stresses that can ultimately lead to illness or even premature death. Life has become a treadmill for many people.

I am sure you know people who seem peaceful and calm, no matter what situation they happen to be in. These fortunate people possess inner peace. Because they are at peace within themselves, every aspect of their life is peaceful. Contrast this with someone who is always stressed out and harassed. That is what is showing on the outside, but it also reveals what is going on inside.

To be most effective at creative visualization you need to seek inner peace and calm. When you are relaxed and peaceful inside, you will be able to concentrate better and achieve much more.

It is a useful, and highly beneficial, exercise to spend some time every day in total silence. You should start with a few minutes and build up to about fifteen minutes every day. This is not as easy as it sounds, but it is worth mastering, as it will make every area of your life more effective. You will find clarity, calm, contentment, and tranquillity in silence. Any decisions you make in this state will be based on strength.

We live in a "doing" society. Everyone is constantly doing things in the hope that these activities will somehow provide inner satisfaction. The risk of this approach to life is that we then define ourselves by what we do, rather than who we are. We are measured by our material accomplishments, rather than who we are inside. This provides nothing more than temporary satisfaction. Wealth and fame are no guarantee of happiness, as the lives of Marilyn Monroe and Kurt Cobain show. There is no point in striving after the visible trappings of success if you feel empty and worthless inside. Lasting happiness never comes from an external accomplishment.

I'm not denying that material achievements aren't important. Of course they are. If no one did anything, nothing would ever be achieved. Even preparing a meal or making a bed is a "doing" activity.

However, greater satisfaction, and ultimately more accomplishment, comes from a "being" approach to life. We have to live with ourselves every day of our lives, and everything we do is motivated by a desire to feel good. Achieving a doing goal provides temporary feelings of euphoria, but it soon fades. When you focus on your inner self you start to change your life from the inside, rather than relying on external stimulus to provide feelings of satisfaction and fulfilment.

This is something that the great religions of the world have tried to teach for thousands of years. The Buddhist teachings of detachment, the teachings of Jesus about loving others, and the Confucian teachings of inner balance all reveal this.

Despite this, many people are scared to think about their inner selves, preferring to fill their lives with constant activity, rather than face the vulnerable person inside.

The ideal scenario is to both be and do, but have the main focus on "be." Allow yourself time off on a regular basis to relax, meditate, and unwind. Enjoy a pleasant walk, have dinner with friends, read a good book, or spend time in the garden. Activities of this sort restore your soul, and put you in touch with the universal mind.

At one time I was a perfect example of a doing person. I felt guilty whenever I took time off for relaxation or pleasure. It took me years to overcome this. Nowadays, I go for a walk every day, meet friends for lunch every now and again, and spend time with my grandchildren. The interesting thing about this is that I achieve more as a result. I am able to return to my work refreshed and revitalized.

Once I stopped trying so hard, and began to nurture myself in this sort of way, my stress levels went down and my productivity went up. It is possible to do less and achieve more.

Another benefit is that new ideas and insights appear when you are relaxed and allow yourself to "be." Often we are so busy that we don't pay enough attention to the thoughts that pass through our minds. We all need quiet times so we can listen to them. I also think that because we are relaxed and receptive, the quality of our ideas improves.

Set aside some quiet time so that you can think about what you want. For this I usually go for a walk, or sit under a favorite tree. You may prefer to have a quiet evening at home. I like to leave the house so that I won't be interrupted. The important thing is that the environment is quiet and you are able to relax. You can do this exercise in many different ways, but I have found two methods that seem to work well with everyone.

Method One

Allow your thoughts to flow freely. Think about what you would like to have, achieve, or accomplish in different areas of your life. Think about your relationships, career, finances, social life, and personal goals. You might want to write down any ideas that occur to you so that you remember them all later. Some people find that they have desires in all areas of their life. Others may have needs in only one or two. It makes no difference how few or how many you have.

Once you have made your list, put it aside for a day or two. I like to carry my list around with me, as other ideas are likely to occur at unexpected moments, and I can add them to the list.

The final part of this preparation stage is to list the items you have written down in order of importance. This sounds easy, but in practice it can be difficult to decide if earning more money is more important than starting a new relationship.

Method Two

Relax in the usual way, and then imagine that you are traveling five years into the future. Once you feel that you are there, think about the work you will be doing five years from now. Do you find it stimulating and absorbing? Have you progressed in your career? What new skills have you developed over the last five years? If you suddenly became a multi-millionaire would you continue to work in the same field?

Imagine yourself leaving work and getting into your car to drive home. What sort of car will you be driving? Are you proud to be seen in it?

Drive home and park your car. Look at your house. Is it in a nice neighborhood? Is it comfortable? Are you proud to invite guests to your home?

Walk inside and walk through the home you will be living in five years from now. Notice the furniture, the ornaments, the paintings, carpets, and drapes. Do you feel relaxed and happy in this environment?

Think about the other people who live with you, and imagine what your relationship with each person will be like five years from now. Are these relationships working the way you want them to be?

In your imagination, drive to wherever you go to achieve personal satisfaction. This could be a hobby, sport, service organization, church, or any other activity that you love. See yourself participating in the activity. If you have gone to a golf club, for instance, see yourself playing a round of golf and noting how much lower your handicap has become in five years.

Return to your home or work again, if you wish to explore these places in greater depth. Visit any other places that you wish, and when you feel ready, open your eyes.

Ask yourself if you are happy with this imaginary tour of your future life. Fortunately, you can change any aspects of it that you do not like. For many people, an experiment like this can be a wakeup call. Think about the experience and then write down your desires for the next five years.

It is important that what you write down excites and motivates you. Everyone wants more money, but if the thought of all the hard work that is required to make that extra money is unappealing, you are not going to carry the goal through to completion.

By the time you have completed these exercises you are likely to have a number of goals. It is possible to use creative visualization techniques to work on several goals simultaneously, but when you are starting out it is better to choose one, and then work on that.

In the next chapter we will discuss why you should dream impossible dreams.

CHAPTER SIX

DREAM THE
IMPOSSIBLE DREAM

"Ask, and it shall be given you."

LUKE 11:9

If you can achieve anything you desire with creative visualization, it stands to reason that you should aim as high as possible. Instead of asking for one thousand dollars for a vacation, why not ask for five or even ten thousand? The answer to this is complicated.

You have tens of thousands of thoughts a day. If most of these thoughts are related to feelings of poverty or worthlessness you are going to find it impossible to use creative visualization techniques to achieve a luxury vacation. Your thoughts have to be in agreement with whatever it is you are visualizing for it to become a reality. Otherwise, you are fighting yourself. You might consciously desire the fabulous vacation at a superb resort, but if your subconscious mind is filled with fears, doubts, and worries about money, or you are so lacking in self-esteem that you don't feel worthy of the vacation, it will not happen.

Fortunately, it is a simple matter to test yourself to see whether or not you should visualize a particular outcome. Sit down comfortably, close your eyes and relax. Think of whatever it is that you would like to achieve. If it is a luxury vacation, think about traveling to your destination in a first-class seat, picture the hotel and the suite you'll be staying in. Think about the sights you intend to visit, and some of the other things you intend to do while on vacation.

Once you have done this, pause and become aware of your body. Is your body reacting positively or negatively to your thoughts? Is your heart pumping with excitement, or is your stomach contracting with fear or uncertainty? Take your time to see if your body is sending you any messages.

The next step is to ask yourself if you are worthy of the luxury vacation. Again, pause to see if your body responds to that thought.

Ask yourself any other questions that relate to the proposed trip. Will you feel guilty about spending that amount of money? Will any other areas of your life suffer as a result of you taking the trip? Would you mind leaving work for the necessary amount of time?

Pause after each question to see if your body reacts in any way. Once you have finished asking questions, take a slow, deep breath and then open your eyes.

By the time you have finished this exercise you should have a clearer picture of how your subconscious mind feels about your desire. If the predominant feeling is one of excitement and anticipation, your subconscious mind will help you achieve this goal. Feelings of nervousness are good, as it shows you are stretching yourself to achieve this goal.

However, if your body reacted negatively in any way, you may need to work on your underlying beliefs before visualizing this particular goal. If, for instance, your stomach, heart, or throat areas tightened at the thought of the money you would spend, you may have subconscious fears about a lack of money. If you received similar responses to your worthiness, you may be suffering from a lack of self-esteem.

Fortunately, there is a remedy to these problems. Stand or sit in front of a mirror, look yourself in the eye, and talk out loud about whatever is holding you back. If your body told you that you were unworthy, for instance, you might say: "I deserve this vacation. I have worked hard for it, and it will do me a world of good. I am worthy of the very best that life has to offer. No one deserves this vacation more than me."

Speak firmly and with expression. When you have finished talking, smile or grin, and then emphasize what you have been saying by concluding with: "Yes, yes, yes!" I like to gesture with my arms, and use as much enthusiasm and energy as possible as I say each "yes."

Wait a few hours and then test yourself again by repeating the first experiment to see what your body has to say. Repeat both exercises until your body gives a positive response to your thoughts. Once you have achieved this, your subconscious mind will be in harmony with your desires and will work on your behalf to help you achieve your goal.

It is important that you aim as high as possible. Your goals should be exciting and daring. They should also make you slightly nervous. Re-evaluate your goals if your body does not react in any way. This means that you might be aiming too low.

Of course, there will be times when whatever it is you are visualizing will be easy to attain. In cases of this sort, you will not need to do the previous exercises. All you need do is start visualizing whatever it is until it becomes manifest in your life.

However, the most exciting visualizations are those in which you stretch yourself and achieve something you would not otherwise have thought possible. In practice, your visualizations are likely to be a mixture of easy, moderate, and demanding goals. You can use creative visualization to achieve anything you desire.

If You Don't Know What You Want

Unfortunately, many people have no idea what they want. They know they want a better life than the one they are currently living, but find it hard to come up with any specific goals. They have no grand dreams, goals, wants, or desires. How can your dreams possibly come true if you don't have any? Of course, everyone has dreams, and there is a remedy if you find it hard to come up with any ideas. Many people have this problem, caused by decades of negative conditioning. There are two ways to overcome this problem. Experiment with both methods and see what comes to you.

Solution One

For the first solution you will need pen and paper. Sit down comfortably and ask yourself what your ideal life would include. Think about what is important to you, and write down anything that makes you feel excited or fulfilled. Think about the possessions you would like to own, and the intangibles, such as overseas vacations or a weekly massage. Consider relationships and health. Think about your ideal career. If you are not happy with the work you are currently doing, make notes of the different types of careers you think would satisfy you.

Think about the changes you would like to make to yourself. Would you like to have more control over your life? How about more energy, increased confidence, a better sex life, improved memory, and better health? How about eliminating some bad habits such as smoking, excessive drinking, and overeating?

You might like to look back over your life and write down the activities you found most enjoyable at each stage. You may find a link between your favorite activities as a child, teenager, young adult, and today. You might also discover a unifying theme if you write down your favorite books, TV programs, and movies.

Write down everything that occurs to you. Do not edit or alter anything. Later on, you'll want to be able to look at the notes you took and read absolutely everything that occurred to you. Start with generalities, and gradually make them more specific. You might, for instance, start with a desire for more money, and then think of the exact annual income you would like to earn. If you want a new car, start by writing that down, but then become specific as to the make, model, and even color of the car you would like.

Once you have completed this process, read your notes out loud and see which ones excite you the most. Choose the idea that resonates most strongly for you, and start using creative visualization to manifest it in your life.

Solution Two

This method uses creative visualization, and is the method I personally prefer. Close your eyes and relax. (Full instructions on how to perform a successful creative visualization session are in the next chapter.) Visualize yourself, ten years from now, relaxing comfortably in a pleasant room. This is a room in the house you'll be living in ten years from now.

Look around the room. Notice every aspect of it. Once you are familiar with the scene, explore the rest of the house. Return to your comfortable chair and enjoy looking around the room again. Notice a coffee table beside you. On it is a magazine with your photograph on the cover. You reach over and pick it up. To your surprise and delight, the magazine is full of articles about you. Some of them look at your home and family life. Others look at your accomplishments. There are also articles about your hobbies, interests, and the vacations you have enjoyed. You see that some of your friends have written articles about you as well. You start reading an article about your typical day. You look at all the photographs, noticing what you are wearing and who is with you. You read another article or two, and then notice a lengthy article about your greatest accomplishment. You read this carefully, noting that it is a totally accurate account.

Once you have read every word in the magazine, you place it back on the coffee table and relax, enjoying the feelings of accomplishment and pride at what you have achieved over the last ten years.

Enjoy the visualization for as long as you wish. When you feel ready to return to the present, take three slow, deep breaths and open your eyes.

After the visualization, write down as much as you can remember. You may not desire everything that came to you during the visualization, but you should be full of ideas that you want to put into practice.

Repeat the visualization as often as you wish. You are in complete control and can change anything about the visualization that you wish. For instance, if you found that you have made little or no progress in the next ten years, you might want to create a totally new scenario. This will give you a huge number of ideas to work on.

It Sounds Okay, But

I am asking you to stretch yourself in this chapter. The natural response to this is to think "It sounds okay, but . . ." and then come up with all the reasons why you cannot have whatever it is you desire. "It sounds okay, but I'm only a clerk. I could never do that." "It sounds okay, but I'm too old." "It sounds okay, but I'd have to complete my degree first."

Listen to all the "It sounds okay, but's" Write them down if you have a long list of them. Look at them all one by one. Are they really as impossible as you think? If they still seem impossible, read Chapter Three again.

There are no real "it sounds okay, but's." All you need is faith in yourself.

Keep Your Visualizations Private

Be careful whom you share your dreams with. Even loved ones may not appreciate what you are trying to do, and try to protect you from something that they think is foolish. Friends and associates may mock your desire to better yourself. They may resent the fact that you are embarked on a program of self-improvement, while they are marking time. They may even be scared that you will leave them behind as you follow your dreams. In practice, I never tell anyone what I am visualizing.

Everything begins with a dream, yet has anyone ever suggested that you dream an impossible dream? Your parents? Teachers? Friends? No one ever suggested it to me, and I think most people would say the same. How can your dreams come true if you don't have a dream in the first place? Do you want to become a millionaire? If so, dream it, visualize it, do whatever else is required, and make it happen. Dreaming is the first step of visualization. Once you have dreamed it, add a healthy dose of passion, and then constantly visualize it until it becomes real.

You have now learned all the essentials. It is time to put what you have learned into action. We will start on this in the next chapter.

CHAPTER SEVEN

CREATIVE VISUALIZATION 101

*"In visualizing, or making a mental picture, you are not endeav-
ouring to change the laws of Nature. You are fulfilling them."*

—GENEVIEVE BEHREND

Now it's time to start on a creative visualization. You have
decided what you want, and your body has responded positively to the idea.

Here are some suggestions to make the visualization as
productive as possible:

- Make sure that you really want whatever it is you are visualizing. The process is unlikely to work if you visualize something because someone told you to do it. Your visualizations must be important to you.

- You cannot use visualization to manipulate or control others. You cannot, for instance, visualize a certain person falling in love with you. That might be what you desire, but it might be the complete opposite of what the other person wants.

- Relax first. Visualization works best when your body is relaxed. In a relaxed state, your brain waves change and become more receptive to suggestions that are put to them.

- There is no need to worry about actually "seeing" whatever it is you are visualizing in your mind. Everyone is different. All you need to do is think about your goal. With practice, you will "see" your visualizations more clearly, but this is not an essential part of the process.

- Use as many senses as possible in your visualizations. If your scene involves you standing in a kitchen, looking out a window, you might smell the newly mown grass, feel the warmth of the sun, taste and smell the freshly baked bread, hear the birds, and also see the beautiful scene you have created. The addition of as many senses as possible increases the power of the visualization.

- Keep your visualizations simple. Experience them as fully as possible, but ideally have a visualization that you can perform in thirty seconds. That way, you can perform a quick visualization session at any time during the day. If you are waiting for someone on the phone, or waiting in line, for instance, you can easily fit in a quick visualization session.

- Ensure that all your visualizations are positive. If you are using creative visualization to help give up smoking, for instance, see yourself walking proudly as a non-smoker, rather than picturing yourself coughing or undergoing nicotine withdrawal. It is highly likely that negative images will come into your mind from time to time when you are visualizing. There is no need to worry about them. Notice them, and let them vanish from your mind.

- Enjoy your visualizations. Sometimes your visualization sessions will go well, while at other times you might feel as if you are not getting anywhere. Take a day or two off from your visualizations whenever you feel you are not progressing. You will return to them with new vigor. Your visualizations should be something you look forward to, rather than a chore.

- Your creative visualizations are mental rehearsals. Consequently, you might like to start your visualizations by thinking about your greatest successes in the past. Think about times when you were supremely confident, and felt good about what you were doing.

Enjoy reliving these positive experiences for a few minutes before starting on your new visualization.

- As much as possible, keep your visualizations to yourself. You do not need the negative comments or resistance that other people, even loved ones, might place in your way.

Your First Visualization

Set aside about thirty minutes and make sure that you will not be disturbed. Once you have gained experience at this, you will be able to do your visualizations in a matter of minutes. However, it is not the length of time they take that is important: It is the energy and belief that you put into your visualizations.

Part One

Sit or lie down comfortably and relax your body using the techniques you learned in Chapter One. You want to be both relaxed and attentive. This is the best state for successful creative visualization, as it quiets logical left-brain activity and allows the creative right brain full scope to create successful images. In addition, a relaxed state allows the visualization to have a greater effect on your nervous system, as it is not competing with any other thoughts, worries, or outside activity.

Part Two

When you feel completely relaxed, start imagining whatever it is you are wanting. If it is an object, such as a new car, you might visualize yourself driving in it, or you might see it in your mind's eye parked outside your home. If it is something less tangible, such as an event, imagine yourself enjoying the occasion, and see yourself acting and behaving in exactly the way you want to. It is important that you experience whatever it is you desire, rather than simply think about it. Include as many details, and as much emotion, as possible.

You might be fortunate and "see" your new car or the event clearly in your mind. You might experience it completely differently, as we all imagine things in our own unique way. Use as many different senses as possible. If you desire a new car, feel the texture of the seat, experience the "new car" smell, see yourself driving down the road in it, and hear the sound of the car's horn as you playfully honk it.

Similarly, if you are visualizing a family get-together on a beach, you might see and hear your relatives, but also feel the texture of the sand beneath your feet, feel the warmth of the sun on your skin, smell the salt air, taste the food, hear the sound of seagulls and the waves crashing on the shore, and maybe see the entire beach in your mind's eye.

Everyone is different. Some people vividly see the beach, while others see very little but hear all the sounds. Others feel the sensation of sand beneath their feet, but may not hear anything.

All you need is your imagination. Imagine yourself in a scene where you are actively participating with whatever it happens to be. If you are requesting a new home, imagine what it will be like. Walk up the drive and in the front door. Walk from room to room, look out the windows, lie down on the beds, and enjoy sitting in a comfortable armchair in the living room. Feel the pride of owning a beautiful home. Experience it all as vividly as you can.

Make the experience fun. You might want to do a handstand in the living room, have a shower with a special friend, or enjoy entertaining family and friends in your new home. You might "hear" background music and pleasant conversation. It makes no difference what is going on, as long as you can imagine it clearly in your mind, and can feel yourself enjoying whatever it is you are using creative visualization for.

In many respects this is a daydream. The major difference is that you are guiding and directing the dream. Usually, daydreams are random images that come into your mind as a result of something that you saw, heard, or thought. Most of the time you have little control over them, and they come and go all day long.

However, in a creative visualization you deliberately focus on something that you desire. You put energy into the process by deliberately choosing what to think about. You are able to add color, sounds, emotion, other people, and pleasant activities to your picture to enrich it further.

Part Three

Before you let your pleasant vision go, you need to affirm to yourself that you are doing whatever it is you desire. If you are visualizing a new car, for instance, you might say to yourself: "I am driving down Santa Monica Boulevard in my brand-new (whatever color, make, and model vehicle you wish) car." If you are visualizing a dream vacation, you might say: "We are sailing down the Rhine River on a beautiful summer's day. We are enjoying looking at the castles and vineyards. This is the most wonderful vacation we have ever had."

As you say these words to yourself, believe that you are, at that very moment, driving the new car, cruising down the river, or being or doing anything else you desire. Feel it, experience it, with as many senses as possible. Allow yourself to be excited, happy, thrilled, and ecstatic. You are celebrating a major achievement. It may not have happened in reality yet, but you know that it will. Believe that it will happen. Jesus told his disciples: "What things soever ye desire, when ye pray, believe that ye receive them, and ye shall have them" (Mark 11:24). In other words, if you believe, you will receive. Consequently, enjoy the entire experience in your mind and know, without a doubt, that you will be successful. Claim whatever it is you desire, and allow yourself to be thrilled and exultant with your success.

Part Four

There is one final step before the visualization concludes. Before you open your eyes, you must say to yourself something along these lines: "I believe that this, or something even better, is coming into my life. It will benefit everyone involved and will bring great joy and happiness. I give thanks to the universe (God, ultimate source, Father, etc.) for bringing these benefits into my life."

When you feel ready, smile to yourself and open your eyes.

As you can see, nothing about creative visualization is complicated or difficult. If necessary, the entire process can be completed in a matter of seconds. I prefer to spend as long as possible thinking about my goal, but if you are exceptionally busy, you may not have enough time to do that.

I normally set aside about half an hour. Usually, I'll use most of that time, but there are occasions when I find it hard to focus on my goal for any length of time. This does not matter. The process of doing this exercise regularly is more important than the length of time each session takes. Repetition is the magic ingredient to success. You need to keep repeating this exercise at least once a day, until you achieve your goal. It is a waste of time to visualize every now and again. It must become a regular part of your life. Five minutes of creative visualization every single day will produce results, but thirty minutes every now and again will probably not. Occasional visualizations are like daydreams. Pleasant, but not particularly productive.

You also need to think about your goal at odd moments during the day. You can create affirmations to help you do this. (We will discuss affirmations in the next chapter.)

You will have noticed that at the end of the visualization you thank the universe for granting your request. Giving thanks in advance is extremely powerful, and eliminates any doubts and fears. You should also thank the universe once your visualization has become a reality.

Secret Room

Some people like to include an additional stage, and perform their visualizations in a special, secret place, either indoors or out. They enjoy the familiarity and security that this imaginary place provides, and allow their visualizations to take place here. I usually visualize a secret room. It is always pleasantly warm, and has a luxurious carpet, comfortable furniture, and some of my favorite possessions on display. I feel comfortable here, and relax instantly whenever I visualize it. This is useful even when I'm not planning a visualization session. If I find myself in a stressful situation, I can imagine my secret room and immediately become calm and relaxed.

To experiment with this, at the end of the relaxation stage imagine a beautiful staircase. Picture and feel the luxurious carpet, and rest one hand on the magnificent banister. In your mind, imagine yourself going down ten steps, while counting backwards from ten to one, and finding yourself inside your own special, secret room.

This room can be anything you wish. It includes your favorite colors, and is always at a comfortable temperature. You already know what my secret room looks like. A friend of mine imagines he is inside a log cabin, as he has always thought how wonderful it would be to live in one. Many years ago, I remember being surprised when a student told me that he imagined himself inside a submarine. Consequently, it makes no difference what sort of room it is, as long as you feel comfortable and relaxed when you are inside it.

You will need a comfortable chair or couch inside the room. Sit or lie down comfortably, look around your room, then close your eyes and start your visualization.

Practice Makes Perfect

Roberto Assagioli, an Italian psychiatrist, created his own system of psychology called Psychosynthesis. He used creative visualization to understand emotional problems, and to achieve personal goals. He devised an interesting experiment to show that people who use creative visualization regularly become better at it, and consequently become even more successful.

His experiment was to imagine a classroom with a blackboard at the front. On the middle of this blackboard is a number written in white chalk. It is large, clear, and easy to read. Let's assume this number is seven. Visualize the blackboard and the number as vividly as possible, and then visualize the number three written on the board on the right-hand side of the number seven. Visualize the seven and three (seventy-three) for a while, and then imagine another number appearing on the right-hand side of the three. Continue doing this until you are unable to visualize the number created by the series of digits.[1]

When you try this exercise you will find that it is not as easy as it may appear. However, with practice, your results will improve, and you will be able to visualize longer sequences of numbers. This experiment shows the control you have over your imagination and will. Dr. Assagioli also pointed out that when the client discovered he or she was making progress, there was a definite motivation to continue.

Incidentally, when Dr. Assagioli experimented with this exercise, he found that extroverted people performed it better with their eyes closed, while introverts frequently did better with their eyes open.

Potential Difficulties

There are a number of potential problems that sometimes concern people who are starting to work with creative visualization.

The first of these is when your mind wanders. This is a common problem, and even people who have practiced these techniques for many years experience it. In fact, a wandering mind is just a factor of life. We all do it. Someone might be telling you something, and you suddenly realize that you missed half of what he or she said because your mind had drifted. You might be attending a lecture, and are fascinated with what the speaker is saying. Even so, the chances are high that you will not hear every word, because your mind will start thinking about all sorts of other things.

Consequently, when you experience this during a creative visualization, realize that it is normal and natural, and that there is no need to berate yourself. Simply start visualizing your goal again, and carry on with the exercise.

A more serious problem occurs when your mind starts sending you negative thoughts about your goal. You might be visualizing a new home, for instance, and suddenly your mind will be full of doubts that you will ever achieve this goal. This might be because you are visualizing something that seems absolutely impossible. If you are currently living in a trailer and are visualizing a multi-million-dollar mansion, it would not be surprising if your mind doubted your ability to achieve this goal. In some cases, you might need to work through the exercises in Chapter Six again. Fortunately, most of the time this will not be necessary. Allow yourself time to think about your doubts and fears, and once you have done this, start visualizing your goal again. It is important that you face up to your concerns. If you ignore them, they are likely to return at odd moments when you are feeling vulnerable, and may cause considerable damage.

Boredom can be a problem, too. Creative visualization should be enjoyable and stimulating. If a particular goal takes a long time to eventuate, it is possible for you to become bored with the visualization. If this occurs, there are two solutions. One is to retain the goal but change the particular visualization, so that you look at the goal from a different angle. Here's an example. Joe was looking for a life partner, and in his visualizations always pictured himself dancing with the woman of his dreams. After a while he started to get bored with this picture. Rather than give up on the visualization, he began seeing himself and his partner in different settings. He visualized the two of them enjoying a picnic, visiting a theme park, attending a movie, eating at a nice restaurant, and participating in a range of other activities. The variety of images enabled him to regain new enthusiasm for the process, and he gradually built up a lengthy list of all the things that he and his partner would do when they finally met.

Another cause of boredom is when you try to focus on a particular scenario for too long. It is better to spend an enjoyable five minutes on the process, rather than force yourself to focus on it for thirty minutes. You should perform the exercise for whatever length of time is enjoyable for you. Sometimes that might be five minutes, while at other times you might enjoy visualizing a particular picture for forty minutes. Ensure that your visualizations remain fun.

Remember that your mind will be inclined to resist change, and consequently the results might take longer than you would like. Sometimes miracles can occur, but usually a creative visualization takes time to bear fruit. Visualization is similar to planting a seed in the ground. You wouldn't plant a seed and then forget about it. You would water it and look after it until it became a full-grown plant. With a creative visualization you plant the thought in your subconscious mind, and then nurture it with positive thoughts and visualizations until it becomes a reality.

CHAPTER EIGHT

AFFIRMATIONS

"A man is what he thinks about all day long."
—RALPH WALDO EMERSON

When I was ten years old I reached the pinnacle of my athletic career. I won the 440-yard race at my school athletics championship. The only reason I won that particular race is that a boy I was competitive with was ahead of me and I was determined to beat him. Consequently, I said over and over to myself as I ran, "I'm going to win, I'm going to win." Quite unknowingly, I was using a positive affirmation.

Affirmations are positive phrases or sentences that are deliberately repeated over and over again to imprint the message into your subconscious mind. Like everyone else, you have thousands of thoughts a day and usually have no idea how many of them are positive and how many are negative. By deliberately inserting positive messages in the form of affirmations, you increase the percentage of positive thoughts that are received by your subconscious mind.

We also have a large number of built-in beliefs about every aspect of our lives. Some of these beliefs are helpful to us in everyday life, while others cause continual problems. A "poor me" attitude, for instance, ensures that you stay "poor," because that is a built-in belief. We can change any unwanted beliefs by using affirmations.

Affirmations work because they create energy, which changes your body and mind at a cellular level. You may think that thoughts are such fleeting things that they cannot possibly affect our minds and bodies in this way. However, medical science has shown that negative thinking over a long period of time can create psychosomatic illnesses.[1]

If negative thoughts can create illness, positive thoughts can produce vibrant health, and virtually anything else we desire strongly enough. Amazing as it may sound, changing our thoughts can change our lives.

Our thoughts also have the power to change others. When you spend any length of time with someone who is angry or unhappy, you are likely to start feeling negative too, because you are picking up and accepting their bad energy. Conversely, when you are with someone who is happy and full of the joys of life, you are likely to express those feelings, also.

A French apothecary and psychotherapist named Emile Coué (1857–1926) came up with a remarkable affirmation at the turn of the twentieth century. His affirmation helped thousands of people, and made him a celebrity. You may already know his all-purpose affirmation: "Every day, and in every way, I am becoming better and better."

Affirmations are always framed in a positive way. It is better to state what you desire, rather than what you wish to avoid. Rather than affirm, "I am going to stop lying," it would be better to say, "I always tell the truth." Likewise, "I'm leaving this town," is not as positive as affirming, "I am living in New York (or wherever you want to be)."

Affirmations are always said in the present tense, as if you already have what you are seeking. Consequently, you might say, "I have a well-paid job that I love," rather than, "I'm looking for a job that pays well, and will be one I love." This is because your subconscious mind does not know the difference between something that is already a reality and something that you want to manifest in your life. By expressing your desire as if it has already occurred, your subconscious mind will immediately start working on making it happen in your life.

Affirmations can be spoken out loud, sung, whispered, said silently, or written down. They need to be said strongly, with feeling, as if they were already a reality in your life. It might seem ridiculous to say, for instance, "I am prosperous," when you are struggling to pay the rent. However, repeating these words regularly will ultimately change your belief system, and once you have done that, abundance will become part of your life.

Whenever possible, I like to say my affirmations out loud, as I can vary the emphasis on different words and put as much expression into my voice as possible. I frequently sing them when driving by myself in the car. When waiting in line at the bank, I repeat my affirmations silently. Incidentally, saying your affirmations is a productive way to use any waiting time. I no longer get annoyed at delays and waits because they give me a chance to say my affirmations. There have even been occasions when the person behind me in the line has told me to move ahead, as I've become so involved in my affirmations that I didn't notice a space becoming available.

Back in the 1920s, Florence Scovel Shinn mentioned a woman who danced while saying her affirmations. "The rhythm and harmony of music and motion carry her words forth with tremendous power," she wrote.[2]

When you say your affirmations, try to visualize a scene that represents the successful accomplishment of your desire. If you are using affirmations to buy a new car, picture yourself driving it. If you desire perfect health, see yourself doing something physical while you say your affirmation. If you desire a partner, see yourself walking hand in hand across a beautiful meadow on a glorious summer's day. If you desire something more abstract, such as more confidence, picture yourself acting confidently in a situation that would have caused difficulty in the past. When you do this you combine a positive visualization with your affirmation.

It is a good idea to spend a few minutes every day saying your affirmations. It is better still to do this at the same time each day. This gives you a chance to say your affirmations in varying ways, and to experiment with new ones that have occurred to you during the day.

I enjoy saying affirmations out loud when I'm driving my car. This is much more productive than listening to commercials on the radio. The other time I especially enjoy saying affirmations is when I'm in front of a mirror. I found this difficult at first, but now I'm used to it, and find saying my affirmations to myself stimulating, positive, and powerful. Try looking at yourself in the mirror and saying something positive and complimentary to your reflection. You might say, "I am a lovable, intelligent person," or simply, "I like myself." Some of my students have told me they had to whisper affirmations like this at first because they were so hard to say. Once you become used to it, you will find saying your affirmations in front of a mirror a highly freeing and exhilarating experience.

Another method that I have found useful is to write your affirmations down. The act of writing your affirmation forces you to focus on the words as you write. Scott Adams, the creator of the highly successful *Dilbert* comic strip, worked as a middle manager at Pacific Bell, but dreamt of becoming a cartoonist. He came up with a powerful affirmation that he wrote down fifteen times a day. He wrote: "I will become a syndicated cartoonist." He noticed changes happening almost immediately, and after many rejections, United Media took him on. Scott Adams still uses affirmations. His current affirmation is: "I will win the Pulitzer Prize."[3]

Generally speaking, affirmations should be short and easy to memorize. Some are general in nature, while others are specific. At the SWAP (Salespeople With A Purpose) Club I belong to, we all say an affirmation at the start and finish of every meeting. It is: "I'm alive, I'm well, and I feel great!" This is a general affirmation that can be used at any time.

If I wanted an affirmation to attract love, friendship, work, money, or health, I would create something specifically for the situation. To attract money, I might say, "I have more money than I need" or "a stream of riches flows into my life all the time." "I have plenty of friends" would help with friendship. A love affirmation would be more difficult, as I would be tempted to include in it some of the qualities I would be looking for in the other person. However, "I enjoy a close, loving relationship with my partner" would be a good start. "I find my work satisfying, stimulating, and enjoyable" might be all that I needed for a work affirmation. However, if I happened to be looking for work in a specific area I would include as much detail about the job I desired as possible. "I enjoy excellent health" is a good affirmation for general health care. Again, I would make it as specific as possible if a particular part of my body was affected. If I was experiencing liver problems, for instance, I might affirm: "My liver is working perfectly, and is looking after me all the time."

You can create affirmations instantly to cover particular situations. An actress friend of mine never suffers from stage fright. However, she unexpectedly panicked one night when she learned that an actress who had auditioned for the part she was playing was in the audience.

"I didn't know what to do," she told me. "It had never happened before. But then I started saying to myself, 'I am peaceful and calm, I am peaceful and calm,' and instantly I felt fine. I gave the performance of my life!"

As you can see, it is not difficult to create simple, yet effective, affirmations that apply specifically to you and your situation. It would be easy to provide you with a list of all-purpose affirmations, but it is better for you to put some thought into it and create your own.

As well as using your own affirmations, you might like to use Scripture passages or lines from favorite poems as affirmations. "I can do all things through Christ which strengtheneth me" (Philippians 4:13) is an extremely popular affirmation.

Norman Vincent Peale recalled traveling in a car with a salesman who had a collection of file cards containing Biblical quotations. He would place them one at a time under a clip on the instrument panel, so that he could meditate and think about them while driving between appointments. From being a negative thinker who made few sales, he became a successful salesman and developed a strong faith at the same time.[4] How could this man possibly fail when he was exposed constantly to affirmations such as, "If ye have faith . . . nothing shall be impossible unto you" (Matt. 17:20) and "If God be for us, who can be against us?" (Romans 8:31).

Once you start using affirmations you will notice that your mind will accept some of them right away, but will reject others. You might say a positive affirmation and immediately receive thoughts objecting to the statement. Surprisingly, it is good for this to happen, as it means one of your long-standing beliefs has been brought to the surface where you can evaluate it and determine if you still need it in your life. Let's say, for example, your mind reacted negatively when you affirmed: "I deserve the very best that life has to offer." As soon as you said this, your mind replied with: "I'm not a very good person. I don't deserve good things in my life." Obviously, this is a sign of low self-esteem, and it is useful to know this. You can use affirmations to gradually improve your self-esteem. Continue saying the affirmation that caused the negative thoughts and notice how they gradually cease to appear. This means that your positive affirmation has replaced the negative thoughts as a belief in your mind.

Daily Affirmations

Whenever I've discussed affirmations in previous books, readers have written to me asking for affirmations they could use. Most of the time, it is better to create your own affirmations that relate to what is going on in your life, and the specific goals you are aiming for. However, there are plenty of general affirmations that can be used by anyone. These affirmations are intended to increase your self-worth and should be said on a daily basis. Here are some examples that you can use as is, or can change to suit your needs. You might adopt all of these, or possibly select a few that seem most useful to you at the moment.

- I create wealth and abundance.
- I am a lovable person.
- I love myself, and others love me.
- I deserve a close, secure, loving relationship.
- I am successful.
- I am happy.
- I am worthy of the best of everything.
- I create joy everywhere I go.
- I deserve the best.
- I give and receive love.
- I attract to myself everything I desire.
- I believe in myself more every day.
- I achieve my goals.

Helpful Hints:

- Your affirmations should always be in the present tense, as if you already have whatever it is you desire. For instance, you might affirm, "My life is rich and abundant," rather than, "I will have a rich and abundant life."

- Your affirmations should be short and easy to remember. Do not include more than one topic in an affirmation.

- Your affirmations should always be phrased in a positive, rather than negative, manner. "I am strong" is better than "I am not afraid."

- Repeat your affirmations as many times a day as possible. Repeat your affirmations to yourself whenever you have a spare moment, such as waiting in line.

- Phrase your affirmations in words that are right for you. By all means use affirmations that you read in books or hear from others, but if necessary, change the wording so that the affirmation sounds as if you created it.

- Your affirmations will be more effective if you are relaxed when you say them. Whenever possible, take a few moments to relax. Lying in bed at night is a good time to say your affirmations, as you are relaxed.

- Whenever you find yourself thinking a negative thought, create an affirmation that affirms the opposite, and repeat it at least twice.

- Say your affirmations to yourself immediately before any situation that concerns you. If you are about to attend a difficult meeting, for instance, say your affirmations before walking in.

- Say your affirmations in different ways. Whisper them, shout them, accentuate different words, sing them. Say them with as much feeling as possible.

- Say your affirmations at different times of the day. Driving in your car, going for a walk, waiting in line, exercising at the gym, or lying in bed at night are all good times to say your affirmations.

Creative Visualization and Affirmations

It can be highly effective to choose an affirmation before starting a visualization session. Once you are relaxed, say the affirmation to yourself and see what symbol or image comes to you. Take particular note of the first impression that comes to you, as that is likely to be the right image for you. Spend a bit of time exploring this image, looking at it from different angles, smelling it, tasting it, and experiencing it in as many different ways as possible. This serves a double purpose. Next time you say the affirmation, the image will also come to your mind, and when you think of the image, the visualization will come back to you. This exercise adds strength and power to the affirmation.

Silent Affirmations

In China, silent affirmations have been used for thousands of years to help encourage and motivate people. For instance, fish are a sign of upward progress. This is because the ancient Chinese observed fish swimming up rivers and leaping up waterfalls to get to the breeding grounds. Consequently, fish tanks, paintings, and ornaments of fish are effective silent affirmations. When a Chinese person sees a fish, he or she immediately thinks of upward progress.

They also use wall hangings with beautiful calligraphy containing words such as "profits increase daily." Naturally, whenever business people read this, they are reminded of their purpose in being at work.

Silent affirmations are an effective way of putting thoughts into your mind at odd moments. You don't need to write your affirmations down and place them on a wall. All you need is something that reminds you of whatever it is you are seeking. If you want to travel, for instance, display a photograph that shows a scene from your destination. If you want a new car, you might be able to display a small photograph of the make and model you desire on your desk.

An acquaintance of mine is a rock musician. He glued photographs of himself playing his guitar onto the covers of music magazines. He also has a photograph gallery on a wall of his bedroom. This displays photographs of every musician he admires, as well as a photograph of himself. Whenever he looks at the photographs, he sees himself in the company of the finest rock musicians in the world.

Each time he picked up the music magazine, he also saw a photograph of himself. These silent affirmations worked well for him, and he has since worked with several of the people who were in his photograph gallery.

Of course, you may not be able to display pictures of everything you want. You may not be able to find suitable pictures, or you may not want other people to know what you are doing. If this is the case, obtain a large scrapbook and paste into it anything that relates to your desires. If you want a new home, for instance, you might find a drawing or photograph of the sort of home you would like. Paste that into your book, and then add any additional information that relates to it. You might write, "four bedrooms, two bathrooms" beside the picture. You might write down the price you are prepared to pay for it. You might insert the desired locality.

If you desire a certain make and model television set, you should be able to find a photograph of exactly what you want. At other times, you might not be able to do this. In these instances, you might choose to draw a picture of what you want, or simply list the essential qualities that you require.

You may not want to use an illustration or photograph for certain desires. If you are looking for a partner, for instance, you will probably choose to list the qualities you desire in that person.

As no one else need see your scrapbook, you can place in it anything at all. You might have dozens of desires.

That's fine. Collect the material you need and paste it into your book. I love searching for photographs and drawings that relate to my desires. The mere act of searching for them forces me to focus on the desire, and this is a form of creative visualization. Even placing them into my scrapbook is a form of ritual, as I am cementing in my desire for whatever it is at the same time as I paste it into the book.

Make your scrapbook as attractive as possible. You might like to add borders or small illustrations to each page. I write positive affirmations at the foot of every page. These are general affirmations that do not necessarily relate to the desire I have illustrated on the page.

You can start using your scrapbook as soon as you have your first desire in it. At least once a day go through the book, looking at the various illustrations and reading the words. Allow yourself to feel excited as you do this. These are all things that you desire, and will ultimately possess.

You can also use your scrapbook at odd moments during the day. Because most of your desires are illustrated with drawings and photographs, you will find that you can easily picture them in your mind. Consequently, you'll be able to mentally go through your scrapbook in your mind, page by page, whenever you have a spare moment during the day.

A friend of mine has devised an interesting silent affirmation that he says works well for him. He places a small bead in his pocket change. Whenever he needs a few coins, he sees the bead and this instantly reminds him of the particular goal he is visualizing. As a bonus, he says that the bead works like a lucky coin and he feels good whenever he has it with him.

One of my students used a rose as a silent affirmation to attract love into her life. Whenever she saw roses anywhere, she immediately thought of her desire to attract the right man. As well as relying on every chance sighting of rose bushes or a rose, she used a mental picture of a rose each time she said her affirmations. The combination of creative visualization, spoken affirmations, and the silent affirmation of a rose worked, as she found the right person in less than six months. Interestingly, this person was also using creative visualization techniques to attract the right person to him.

In fact, you can use anything at all to act as a silent affirmation. An acquaintance of mine automatically says his affirmations to himself whenever he exercises. The gym he goes to has become the trigger that immediately reminds him of his affirmations. He also likes the fact that he is gaining at least double the benefit by exercising at the same time as he repeats his affirmations. The only disadvantage is that he has to repeat them silently, rather than saying them out loud.

Writing Your Affirmations

It can be a useful exercise to write an affirmation down on a sheet of paper, and then follow this by writing down all the thoughts that occur to you as a result. You may find that your responses are not what you expected. Sometimes you might write down a negative comment about an affirmation that you thought your mind had welcomed and accepted. At other times, an affirmation that you thought might be resisted by your mind will receive positive comments when you write it down.

Obviously, you should think about any negativity that crops up, and possibly create some new affirmations to deal with it. If you repeat this exercise on a weekly basis, you will notice your responses will gradually change to reflect what is going on in your mind.

The other benefit of writing your affirmations down is that you are forced to focus on them while in the process of writing. You also see the affirmation in written form, and ultimately you think about what you have written. This is a powerful way of strengthening the effectiveness of your affirmations.

CHAPTER NINE

OVERCOMING PERSONAL PROBLEMS

*"There is a law in psychology that if you form a picture
in your mind of what you would like to be, and you keep and hold
that picture there long enough, you will soon become exactly
as you have been thinking."*

—WILLIAM JAMES

Everybody has limitations on what they can achieve. Some
of these cannot be changed. It's impossible to change one's
height, for instance. However, creative visualization techniques can be used to eliminate many perceived limitations. Confidence and self-esteem are good examples.

Many people are crippled with a poor self-image that holds them back in every area of their lives. Creative visualization enables them to eliminate this and make amazing changes in their lives. Creative visualization can also eliminate negative thinking, enabling its sufferers to gain a more positive approach to life. It can even be used to help people lose weight and affect other life-changing decisions.

Many addictions can be cured with the power of creative visualization. Smoking is a good example. However, people are addicted in varying degrees, and consequently, depending on the addiction, many people need professional help as well. Even in these cases, creative visualization can play a useful role in helping to free the person from the addiction.

The most common personal problems involve low self-esteem. Shyness, nervousness, lack of confidence, and numerous behavioral problems are outward indications of this. Consequently, there are few people who wouldn't benefit from using creative visualization techniques to bolster their self-esteem.

Holly came to me for help because she found it difficult to say "no." Consequently, she frequently found herself doing things that she would rather not. One evening, a week before she came to me, a young man had phoned her and invited her out. She told me that she became flustered and agreed to go out with him, even though she wanted to say no. It was a simple matter to have her visualize a similar scenario in the future. She visualized herself giving the response that she desired, either accepting or turning down the invitation. By practicing this, Holly was relaxed and in control when the situation occurred again.

Like so many things, Holly's inability to turn down an unexpected invitation was related to her self-esteem. From now on, every time she gives the response that she desires, her self-esteem will increase along with her happiness.

Self-Esteem Exercise

- Think of a situation or scenario that causes you difficulty. It makes no difference what it is.

- Relax in the usual manner.

- Say to yourself several affirmations that relate to self-esteem. You might say some of these: "I am a worthwhile human being;" "I am worthy of the very best that life has to offer;" "I am confident in every type of situation;" "I like myself;" "I am glad to be me;" "I am achieving my goals."

- Visualize yourself in a situation that would be difficult for you. This might be a scene from your past, or you might choose to imagine a situation that would be hard for you to handle.

- Observe the scene for several seconds, and then allow all the color to fade away from your mental picture until you are looking at the scene in black and white.

- Allow this black-and-white picture to gradually become smaller and smaller, as if it is receding into the distance. When it is little more than a dot in your mind's eye, visualize the scene again the way you would like it to be. Allow this scene to be in glorious color, and see, hear, feel, taste, and smell the picture in your imagination. See yourself performing everything you need to do with ease, enjoying every moment.

- Allow the black-and-white scene to come back into your mind for a few seconds, and then replace it with the second scene. Notice the total transformation you have made between the two scenes. Repeat this several times, observing the "old" you and the "new" you.

- The final stage of this exercise is to totally eliminate the old black-and-white picture. You can do this in various ways. I sometimes allow the old scene to turn into a small ball which I can kick into the air. I watch it ascend into the air and finally disappear. You might visualize a trash can. Turn the black-and-white scene into a small parcel that you can pick up. Dump it into the trash can and replace the lid.

- Once the old picture has gone, visualize the new scene again. Enjoy watching it for as long as you wish. When you feel ready, open your eyes.

- Repeat this exercise as often as you can until the second picture becomes a reality in your life.

Patterns of Behavior Exercise

This exercise is similar to the previous one, and is used to change long-standing habit patterns. Just recently, a client of mine used this exercise to lose forty pounds. The affirmation she used along with this exercise was: "I'm lithe, slim, and athletic." It took her almost six months to achieve this goal, but today she is definitely lithe, slim, and athletic.

Another client of mine used this exercise to eradicate a gambling addiction. Her affirmation was: "I enjoy spending money wisely."

Salespeople have used this exercise to overcome call-reluctance and fear of rejection. All sorts of fears have been overcome by this simple exercise. A young man I know wanted to invite a girl to a party, but was too scared to make the initial contact. This exercise enabled him to overcome his fear, and he and the girl are now engaged.

- Think about the fear or pattern of behavior that is affecting your life.

- Relax in the usual manner.

- Say some affirmations that relate to the problem.

- Think about the most recent situation when you exhibited the behavior pattern you want to change. Visualize it in your mind as clearly as possible. Look at it dispassionately. If you sense any emotion building up inside you, pause and take several slow, deep breaths before continuing.

- Let go of that picture and go back to an earlier time when you demonstrated the same behavior. Again, look at it calmly and dispassionately. Once you can see it clearly in your mind, let it go, and go back to a still earlier instance. Keep on doing this until you can go back no further.

- Look at the earliest instance you can recall in which you demonstrated the behavior or activity you want to change. Notice how much younger and immature you were then.

- Let go of that picture and return to the present. Remain relaxed, with your eyes closed. Take three slow, deep breaths and then project yourself into the future. See yourself in a scene in which you would have normally exhibited the behavior you want to change. However, this time see yourself assertive and in total control. See yourself acting in a mature, confident manner. If you want to ask a certain person out, see yourself doing it in a natural, pleasant way. If you want to eliminate problem foods from your diet, see yourself selecting good, healthy food from a large selection. See yourself showing no interest at all in the foods you craved in the past. No matter what the change you want to make, see yourself doing it happily, with no regrets or anxiety.

- Congratulate yourself on making the change. Allow feelings of pride and pleasure to wash over you.

- Return to the very earliest scene you can remember. Mentally say goodbye to it. Allow it to fade from view and be replaced with the future scene. Tell yourself that this is the way it will be from now on.

- Observe the future scene for as long as you can. Enjoy the sights, sounds, tastes, smells, and feelings that come to you.

• When you feel ready, smile to yourself, and open your eyes.

Creating a Script

You might find it helpful to create a script to reinforce your goal. This is called a guided visualization, because the script directs and guides your thoughts. Scripts can be created for almost any purpose. Just recently, I helped a woman overcome her fear of flying with a guided visualization script that she played over and over again until her phobia disappeared.

The first step is to create a script for whatever it is you desire. These scripts are in three parts: relaxation, the message, and returning to the present. I find fifteen to twenty minutes is about the right length for a guided visualization. Most people speak about 150 words a minute. Consequently, the script you prepare should be no longer than 3,000 words.

Think about the problem you are concerned with, and write the script with your desired outcome in mind. Try to include as much emotion and feeling as possible. Here is a sample script that I wrote for someone who wanted more confidence:

Self-Confidence Script

"Take a nice, deep breath in and allow your eyes to close as you exhale slowly. Feel a pleasant wave of relaxation drifting into every part of your body. It is so pleasant and so comfortable to simply relax and allow all the strains and tensions of the day to fall away from you.

"Take another deep breath in now, and, as you exhale, let another wave of relaxation drift over you from the top of your head all the way down to the tips of your toes. Just enjoy this pleasant feeling of total relaxation. Muscles relaxing more and more with each easy breath you take.

"You will notice that every breath you take makes you more and more relaxed, more and more relaxed. You are becoming loose, limp and so, so relaxed as you drift deeper and deeper into a state of total relaxation.

"Just become aware of the muscles around your eyes now, and let those muscles relax. Feel the relaxation as it gradually moves into every part of your body, taking you to a deeper, even more tranquil state than ever before.

"Allow yourself to float deeper and deeper into a pleasant, relaxed, tranquil state where nothing need bother or disturb you. Each breath allows you to go deeper and deeper and deeper.

"Any outside sounds will not disturb or distract you. In fact, they'll help you go deeper and deeper and deeper into a state of total relaxation.

"Become aware of your toes now, and let them relax. Allow the relaxation from your toes to drift into your feet, so now both feet become totally relaxed. Totally relaxed and limp. And now allow that relaxation to drift up both legs. Feel your calves and knees and thighs relaxing more and more with each easy breath you take. And as you relax you feel yourself going deeper and deeper into this pleasant, tranquil, relaxed state where nothing need bother or disturb you.

"Feel the relaxation drifting into your stomach and up into your chest. It feels so wonderful to be totally relaxed like this. Allow the relaxation to drift into your shoulders now. That's good. That's very good. And now feel the relaxation drifting down your arms, all the way to the tips of your fingers. Just relaxing, relaxing, relaxing. . . (Pause)

"Allow the relaxation to drift into your neck and face, right on up to the top of your head, so that you're completely relaxed from the tips of your toes to the very top of your head.

"It feels so comfortable to rest like this, just loose and limp and so, so relaxed. It's a wonderful sensation, so restful, tranquil, peaceful, and calm. Just quietly listening to the sound of my voice as you go deeper and deeper into perfect, total relaxation.

"Completely let go now as you allow this wonderful, restful relaxation to drift and spread right through every single nerve and cell of your body.

"Mentally scan your entire body now to see if any areas are still tight or tense. Focus in on them and allow them to relax, just as much as the rest of your body. You feel so comfortable now. Totally relaxed in every part of your body. You have no desire to do anything except wait for the suggestions that will help you gain all the confidence you desire.

"Your breathing is slow and steady as you drift deeper and deeper into this wonderful world of total relaxation. You want to be in the deepest state you can, as it is so beneficial for you, with every particle of your being feeling totally relaxed.

"It's a wonderful feeling to be so relaxed and comfortable, with nothing to disturb or bother you. You feel warm, secure and so, so limp and relaxed. This pleasant sensation is so peaceful and so relaxing. You feel wonderfully relaxed, but you know you can go even deeper into a state of complete and total relaxation.

"Just picture yourself now at the top of a beautiful staircase. It is the most beautiful staircase you have ever seen. You can feel the luxurious carpet beneath your feet, as you look down this gorgeous staircase. There is a magnificent room down there, full of people you love, and who love you. You can hear the happy conversation drifting up the staircase, and you decide to go down to join them.

"You place your hand on the highly-polished handrail now, and together we'll go down the ten steps to join the happy group in the room below. As I count from ten down to one, you'll allow yourself to double your relaxation with each step as we slowly make our way down.

"Ten. Double your relaxation as we take the first step down this magnificent staircase.

"Nine. Another step and again doubling your relaxation. Drifting down, deeper and deeper.

"Eight. Drifting down still further as you take another step and double your relaxation once more.

"Seven. Totally limp, loose and relaxed, as you take another step.

"Six. Doubling your relaxation once more.

"Five. We're halfway down this beautiful staircase, and we pause and look around at the happy scene as you double your relaxation once again.

"Four. Becoming so totally relaxed.

"Three . . . two . . . and one.

"As you step off the staircase and join the happy people in the room, you double your relaxation once again, and now you're totally, absolutely, loose, limp, and relaxed. (Pause)

"You're enjoying the company of this room full of happy people. They are all people whom you know well, and it surprises you to find them all together in the same room. There are people here from your earliest school days, and friends whom you haven't seen for years. There are former neighbors and curent friends. Some of your favorite relatives are here too, even some who died years ago, but they are all looking exactly as you knew them, and they are all thrilled to see you.

"They tell you that they have come here to see you, as you are so special and important to them. They surround you with friendship, love, and incredible confidence. You realize that with their faith and support you really can achieve anything. They fill you with confidence and inner strength and a feeling of total well-being, knowing that you can accomplish anything you set your mind to, anything at all. They urge you to aim high and to take total control of your life. Their faith and confidence in you makes you realize that, yes, you can achieve anything you set your mind on. It seems strange that all these people have more confidence in you than you used to have in yourself. But you know now that you can achieve anything, and you are motivated and determined to succeed, to cast aside the shackles that tied you down and to become the glorious, successful, confident, motivated person that is the real you.

"In your mind's eye now, think back to a scene from your past where your confidence let you down, or you felt that you had not made a good impression. Look at this scene in a detached way, almost as if it is on a small black-and-white television screen and is happening to someone else, rather than you. Watch this scene, and now go through it again, but this time it is entirely different as you have all the confidence that you lacked before. This time see yourself doing everything in a relaxed, confident manner. Notice the wonderful impression you make. Feel the confidence within you as you relive this scene. Feel how poised and happy you are. Notice the wonderful response other people have toward you. Observe all the fine details.

"Now, go through this second scene once more, the one where you felt so confident, but this time see it on a huge screen, in glorious color. Feel and sense and see every aspect of that scene, and feel good about yourself, because you know that this is how you are going to be from this moment on. (Pause) You are a confident, worthwhile human being. You deserve all the good things of life and you are making them happen, from this moment on. Allow this confidence to filter through every nerve, muscle, and fiber of your being, revitalizing and restoring yourself.

"You are so happy now. You have thrown off the cloak of shyness, timidity, and insecurity and are revealing your true, confident, inner self. Everything you do from now on will be as the real, confident you. You have no use for that old, tattered cloak that held you back and revealed nothing of the wonderful and real you inside.

"From now on, you will be in total control of your life. You have total control over your thoughts as well as your actions. From now on you'll be alert to the insidious negative thoughts that sometimes manage to creep into our conscious awareness. Whenever you find yourself thinking a negative thought, you'll simply replace it with a positive thought. You may switch the negative thought around completely, or perhaps replace it with a positive affirmation. As your mastery over your thoughts increases, so will your confidence, vitality, and happiness. You are a positive, enthusiastic person who looks on the bright side of everything. Disappointments and setbacks will no longer bother or disturb you. You will simply regard them as learning opportunities that open doors for further progress.

"You will no longer be content to lead a life in the shadows. You deserve your place in the sun, and you are going to claim it. Every now and again you'll move out of your comfort zone to maintain your rightful position in the sunshine. We all need to stretch ourselves every now and again, and you'll derive enormous pleasure out of doing this. Each time you stretch yourself in this way your confidence will increase. You have the power, the energy, the enthusiasm, and the confidence to overcome any obstacle that stands in the way of your success. You are in complete control of your own life and you choose to lead life as a confident, secure, positive, happy person.

"Visualize yourself now, in the near future, in a situation that would have caused you difficulty in the past. See yourself doing it all with effortless ease and total confidence. That is the real you, and from now on it is the real you that you'll display to the world. As you do this, your achievements will become greater and greater, your happiness will expand, your relationships with everyone will improve, and you'll feel in total control of every aspect of your life.

"You are a totally confident person and you can do anything you set your mind on. You are a totally confident person.

"As your confidence continues to grow and expand you'll find your relationships with others will also improve. You are sympathetic, supportive, and understanding. Because of what you have been through, you realize that other people also have problems and difficulties in their lives, and you enjoy helping them. Your friendly smile, sympathetic nature, and confident manner help other people to recognize their own worth, and they like you the more for being prepared to listen and understand.

"Your sense of humor is growing daily. Things that would have bothered you in the past are no longer important, and you can laugh at small setbacks. Every time you smile or laugh you are expressing your special warmth and love to the world. Your smile has the power to change lives, and you find yourself smiling and laughing more than ever before. Each time you do this your confidence and self-esteem expand.

"And as you drift even deeper into pleasant relaxation you realize that you are unique and important. What you think, feel, and say are just as valuable and important as the thoughts, feelings, and conversation of anyone else. You are important and valuable, and you celebrate your own individuality. You no longer care what other people say or think. You are confident and secure and worthy of the very best that life has to offer.

"You are confident that you can do anything you set your mind on. You see yourself as a successful, happy, secure, and supremely confident person. Because you feel good about yourself, every day is going to get better and better. You deserve to be successful, and because you are confident and in total control, you are going to make the future even more successful than the present.

"And now we are going to return to the present on the count of five. When I reach five, you'll open your eyes feeling absolutely wonderful. You'll also open your eyes filled with unlimited, total confidence.

"If you are listening to this tape in bed at night, at the count of five you'll be able to roll over and fall sound asleep, sleeping soundly until it is time to wake up in the morning. Any other time you are listening to this tape, you'll open your eyes at the count of five feeling wonderful in every possible way.

"Now the counting begins. One, gaining energy, feeling wonderful. Two, coming up now, feeling a wave of confidence surge through every pore of your being. Three, becoming aware of the situation in the room. Four, feeling totally revitalized and better than you've felt in a long, long while. And five, eyes opening, and feeling wonderful."

There are two ways you can use a script of this sort. You can record it onto a cassette tape and play it back whenever you wish. Alternatively, you can familiarize yourself with the contents of the script and then silently repeat it to yourself while you are relaxed. I prefer to record the script, as it keeps me focused on the purpose of the guided visualization. However, it is not always practical to do this, and I find it helpful to remember the main points of the guided visualization so I can run through it in my mind when lying in bed at night, or whenever I have some free time.

I always record my own guided visualizations. I have heard that it is better to have the messages recorded by someone of the opposite sex. However, depending on the nature of the problem, you may not want to have the contents of your tape known to anyone else. Also, it is usually more convenient to simply record a new tape for yourself, rather than waiting until someone else is available to record it for you.

Guided visualizations work well on their own, but are especially effective when used in conjunction with affirmations and creative visualizations.

CHAPTER TEN

SELF-IMPROVEMENT

To lead a full and worthwhile life, we should constantly be seeking to improve ourselves in as many ways as possible. We can continue our education, take up new interests, develop talents, improve our social skills, improve our memory, and work on becoming the person we desire to be five or ten years from now.

Creative visualization can play a major role in all areas of self-improvement. Realizing your potential and working on a program of self-development is one of the most satisfying aspects of life. It is highly satisfying to know that you are better today than you were yesterday, thanks to your own efforts.

Have you ever met someone who felt that he knew everything, and consequently needed to make no effort to improve himself further? Unfortunately, there are many people like this. Once a person reaches this stage, he is old, no matter what his chronological age might be. Continuing to learn is one of the best ways to remain young and interested in life.

My late friend, Walter, took up printing in his sixties and computing in his seventies. The final twenty years of his life were amongst his happiest as he learned more and more about his new interests. On the day he died he enrolled on a new programming course. Right up to the day he died at the age of 83, he was as enthusiastic as a teenager. He credited his youthfulness to the fact that he was always learning. Walter demonstrated the truth that the more you learn, the more capable you become of further learning.

Everyone has time for self-improvement. A former neighbor of mine taught himself Russian. He had no plans to travel there, but learned the language as an intellectual exercise. He had less free time than most people, but learned the language by playing cassettes in his car, studying for ten or fifteen minutes in the evening, carrying flash cards around with him, and by using every spare moment he could find visualizing himself speaking fluent Russian. Whenever possible, he would close his eyes to make the visualization as vivid as possible, but he even learned to do it with his eyes open. This enabled him to use creative visualization while waiting in line, and even while waiting for traffic lights to turn green.

When I asked him why he was learning something that was unlikely to be useful to him, he replied that it was the intellectual stimulation he enjoyed, and that with motivation he could achieve virtually anything.

Motivation is obviously a key ingredient in creative visualization. You would not create the time to visualize your goals unless you were motivated to achieve them.

You will find that you will achieve your self-improvement goals more quickly and with much less effort when you incorporate creative visualization into the process. I would recommend that you allow enough time to do a complete creative visualization exercise whenever possible. However, there is no reason why you could not seize odd moments during the day for thirty-or sixty-second visualizations instead, or as well.

Not long ago, a young man came to me for help. He was in danger of losing his job as a car salesman because he was not making any sales. Myles had a friendly, outgoing personality, and loved cars. However, he lacked the confidence required to ask for the order. As he was paid on a commission basis, he was suffering financially, also. If he didn't turn his dismal sales record around quickly, he'd have to find other employment. The main problem was his self-esteem, but Myles also needed to develop some sales skills.

On our first meeting, I asked Myles to tell me exactly what he wanted. Not surprisingly, his answer was that he wanted to sell more cars. I then asked him to write down all the steps that were involved in the process from the moment a prospect entered the showroom. After about ten minutes, Myles came up with a list:

- Prospect walks in.
- I introduce myself, and ask how I can help.
- I listen carefully, to determine the prospect's needs. I determine if financing would need to be arranged to secure the sale.
- I then show prospect the cars that I think would be best suited to him or her.
- I explain the features of each car, and also the benefits that the prospect would gain from each one.
- I encourage the prospect to have a test drive in the cars they like best.
- I ask them to tell me about each car, after they have had a test drive.
- Prospect decides which car he or she likes best.
- We determine if the prospect can afford the car.
- I ask for the sale.
- We prepare a sale agreement.
- Client—no longer a prospect—drives away in new car.
- I follow up several times to ensure that client is happy with the purchase. I establish a long-term relationship with client, as I want to sell him or her many cars in the future.

I then asked Myles to relax and visualize the entire process in his mind, seeing and experiencing every step of the process. Myles was a good visualizer and had no difficulty in following the process from start to finish.

I then asked him to close his eyes, and mentally go through the first stage once more. Once he had done this, I asked him to keep his eyes closed, while I asked him if he felt any negative sensations at all in his body or mind while experiencing it. He hadn't. In fact, the only feelings he had were positive.

After this, I asked him to visualize all of the stages, one by one. Myles admitted feeling slightly nervous at stage two when he had to introduce himself to the prospect. Stages three to nine were all positive. Myles was knowledgeable about his product and enjoyed discussing cars. On stage ten (asking for the sale), Myles felt a knot in his stomach. However, he felt positively elated on steps eleven to thirteen.

I suggested that Myles write down several positive affirmations about himself and sales. I explained that his job was to provide his clients with the best car they could afford. He should be proud to have the opportunity to sell a good product to them. Somehow, Myles had developed negative feelings about selling, and this, combined with a slight lack of confidence, was depriving him of a livelihood, and his potential clients of a good car.

None of this was surprising, but it showed Myles the areas he needed to work on. After some thought, he came up with several affirmations:

- "I enjoy selling cars."
- "I am a responsible and successful salesperson."
- "I enjoy helping my customers."
- "I gain satisfaction from helping my clients buy the right car for their needs."
- "I am an honest and ethical salesperson."
- "I like people, and enjoy welcoming potential clients."

Myles practised his visualizations first thing every morning, and again before he went to bed at night. He enrolled in a basic selling course, and repeated his affirmations as frequently as he could.

At least once a week, Myles tested himself on each stage of the selling process to see what his body and mind had to tell him. It took three weeks for his body to feel at ease on all thirteen steps. By that time, his sales had improved markedly, and he and his fiancé were able to start talking about buying their own home.

Although Myles is now a successful car salesman, he still practices his visualizations twice a day. He also mentally replays sales situations that did not turn into sales, to determine what he could have done differently to achieve a successful result. In his morning visualizations, Myles always sees a plentiful supply of prospects coming into the showroom, and he experiences every moment of his time with each one. Although he would not call himself psychic, on a number of occasions Myles has "seen" people in his mind hours before they walked into his showroom.

"They are the easiest ones to sell," he told me. "I've already sold to them once in my mind. That means they're clients rather than prospects. Somehow knowing that means the whole process goes exactly as it did in my mind."

Myles used creative visualization to improve his selling skills. He is now also using it to improve his golf game. (Using creative visualization for sports is the subject of the next chapter.)

Self-Improvement in Your Secret Room

The secret room that we discussed in Chapter Seven can be utilized in many ways for self-improvement purposes. First of all, decide what area of your life you wish to work on. Let's assume that you want more self-confidence. Relax, and then visualize yourself inside your secret room. Think about someone you know who has plenty of confidence, and invite him or her into your room. Ask your guest to take off his or her shoes, and then step into them. You will find you suddenly have all the confidence that the other person has. Walk around the room in your guest's shoes, and allow yourself to enjoy the feelings of supreme self-confidence in every cell of your body. Once you feel that the confidence has permeated through your entire body, take off the shoes and return them. You return the shoes, but you keep the confidence. Say goodbye to the person and then relax for as long as you wish in your secret room, happy because you now have all the confidence that you lacked before. When you feel ready, return to your everyday life.

You can use this technique to gain any quality that you desire.

CHAPTER ELEVEN

SUCCESS AT SPORTS

"When the mind talks, the body listens. We literally talk ourselves into and out of every victory or defeat in the game of life."

—Dr. Denis Waitley

Creative visualization is an extremely effective tool that will help you to achieve the best you are capable of, both in training and in competition. Many champion athletes have spoken about the benefits of creative visualization. Terry Orlick, a sports psychologist and former gymnastics champion, wrote: "Most of our Olympic and world champions do at least 15 minutes of imagery daily, and many regularly do an hour or so each day when preparing for major competitions."[1] If most world champions use creative visualization to achieve excellence, imagine what it could do to your game or sport.

Have you ever watched Tiger Woods studying an important shot before hitting the ball? He was visualizing the ball going exactly where he wanted it to go. His father, Earl, taught him how to use creative imagery when he was just a boy. Tiger Woods is just one of countless athletes who use creative visualization to achieve sporting prowess. Examples of famous athletes who use creative imagery include Michael Jordan (basketball), Jean-Claude Killy (skiing), Jack Nicklaus (golf), Nancy Kerrigan (figure skating), Michelle Davison (diving), and Janet Dykman (archery).[2] On one occasion, Jean-Claude Killy was injured and could not physically prepare for his next race. However, he skied the course mentally in his mind, and when it came time to race, produced one of his best results.

Jack Nicklaus provided a powerful description of how he used creative visualization: "First, I see the ball where I want it to finish, nice and white and sitting up high on the bright green grass. Then the scene changes and I *see* the ball going there: its path, trajectory, and shape, even its behavior on landing . . . the next scene shows me making the kind of swing that will turn the previous images into reality."[3] Here's another quote from Jack Nicklaus, possibly the greatest visualizer in sport: "Before every shot I go to the movies inside my head. Here's what I see. First I see the ball where I want it to finish in a specific small area or fairway or green. Next I see the ball going there—its path, trajectory, and behavior on landing. Finally I see myself making the kind of swing that will turn the first two images into reality. These 'home movies' are a key to my concentration and to my positive approach to every shot."[4]

People have been discussing the mind game of golf for at least one hundred years. The old cliché, "Golf is 99% mental," probably dates back that far, as well. In his book, *The Mystery of Golf*, published in 1908, Arnold Haultain wrote: "To play golf well a man must play like a machine; but like a machine in which the mental-motor must be perfect as the muscular mechanism."[5]

Mark McGwire told *The New York Times* that he used visualization techniques to hit seventy home runs during the 1998 baseball season. His technique was simple. "I visualized my bat making contact with the ball," he said.[6]

Danni Roche was a member of the Australian hockey team that won a gold medal at the Atlanta Olympics. She did her visualizations in the shower after training. She saw herself, and the rest of the team, on the dais receiving a gold medal. In her visualizations, Korea always came second. Interestingly enough, that is exactly what happened. Standing on the dais, Danni Roche said to her colleague Karen Marsden, "I'm not sure if it's real or if it's another dream."[7] She had visualized this outcome so many times that she almost had to pinch herself to make sure that it was real.

Herb Elliott, the great Australian athlete, ran the sub-four-minute mile seventeen times. He won the gold medal for the 1500 meters at the 1960 Rome Olympics. One of the techniques he used was to visualize a competitor on his shoulder. This was an imaginary, faceless, nameless person who was waiting to pass Herb at a suitable moment. This picture kept Herb from slowing down each time the little, insistent voice in his head suggested he could ease off slightly.[8]

Brian Orser, the 1987 world champion in men's figure skating, felt, rather than "saw," his visualizations. "My imagery is more just feel," he wrote. "I don't think it is visual at all. I get this internal feeling. When I'm actually doing the skill on the ice, I get the same feeling inside."[9]

Carl Lewis, the great track star, always visualized himself winning the race while preparing to start. Greg Louganis, the Olympic-gold-medal-winning diver, "mind-scripted" each dive some forty times before performing it. Some of these visualizations were in slow motion, while in others he pictured the dive in real time.[10]

It is not hard to see why most athletes use creative visualization. If you imagine you are running in a race, for instance, your heart will start beating harder, even though the race is occurring only in your mind. This shows how closely creative visualization and performance are connected. In fact, researchers in Lyons, France, have discovered that good visualizers make much better athletes than their colleagues who cannot or do not visualize.[11] While visualizing, these top athletes also experience the same feelings and sensations in their bodies that they receive when competing. They feel the anxiety, stress, and excitement of the competition. They use all of their senses. They picture the stadium and mentally achieve the correct body position for every move. They feel the ball in their hand, smell the freshly mown grass, hear the bat hit the ball, and see it soar up into the air, going exactly where they want it to go. They hear the roar of the crowd and taste the joys of success.

Edmund Jacobson was a psychologist and physiologist who developed the technique of progressive relaxation in the 1930s. He discovered that people's muscles showed a measurable amount of the same electrical activity that they produced in movement when the subjects imagined themselves doing a specific activity.[12]

In the 1960s, Alan Richardson, an Australian psychologist, conducted an experiment to determine how effective creative visualization techniques could be for athletes. He selected three groups of basketball players who had not used creative visualization before. The first group practiced their free throws every day for twenty days. At the end of this time they had improved by 24 percent. The second group did no practice for twenty days. Not surprisingly, their results did not improve. The third group did not pick up a basketball for the whole twenty days. However, every day they visualized themselves making free throws. They improved 23 percent, only one percent lower than the first group who had practiced on a court with real hoops and balls.[13] This has since become a standard experiment in college psychology classes all around the world.

Creative visualization is particularly useful in helping you focus on areas of your game or sport that need improvement. For instance, if you find that you constantly slice the ball when playing golf, your coach would show you the correct swing. You would practice this until you got it right, and could then perfect the swing in your mind using creative visualization. However, you need to be careful to use only positive visualizations. If you practice the incorrect swing in your mind, your game will get worse.

This can be a problem for some athletes. Naturally, they are not going to win every event they take part in. If they focus on their defeats, rather than their successes, they program themselves for failure the next time they compete. The solution to this problem is for them to visualize themselves playing at their very best and achieving success. Repeating positive visualizations of this sort over and over again provides positive reinforcement and increases the chances of winning next time.

The most astonishing example of creative visualization I have heard of concerned a keen golfer who did not play a round of golf for seven years. However, he played a game every single day in his mind. When he finally walked onto a golf course again, he cut twenty strokes off his normal game.

Major James Nesmeth did not deliberately stay away from the golf course. He spent seven long years as a prisoner of war in North Vietnam, confined to a cage that was five feet long and four-and-a-half feet high. For seven years he saw hardly anyone and was unable to enjoy any form of physical activity. After a few hopeless months, praying to be released, Major Nesmeth decided that he had to do something with his mind to retain his sanity. He chose to play a complete round of golf in his mind. Every day for the next seven years he imagined himself dressed in his golfing clothes, and playing eighteen holes at an exclusive country club. He experienced all the sights, sounds, and smells he would have sensed if he had actually been there. He saw birds flying overhead, saw squirrels in the branches of the trees, felt the rain and wind on his face on wintry days, and chose the different clubs he needed for his game. He felt and experienced every detail of every shot he made. Each game was played in real time. As Major Nesmeth couldn't go anywhere, he was able to experience a leisurely round of golf every day. In his mind's eye, he saw every single shot landing exactly where he wanted it. After seven years of mental practice, Major Nesmeth not only had kept his sanity, he had improved his normal golf score by twenty strokes.

I am not suggesting that you become a hermit for seven years. However, if you visualize yourself playing your favorite sport in the detail that Major Nesmeth did, your game will inevitably improve. His experience shows that creative visualization is just as good as playing an actual game when you are unable to play for any reason. If you are tired or injured, for instance, you can still continue training in your mind. If the correct equipment is not available, or the weather is inclement, or circumstances prevent you from playing, you can still practice in your mind. If you are playing a team sport, you can practice by playing imaginary games in your mind, without the necessity for all the other members of the team to be present.

One of the main benefits of using creative visualization, in addition to playing the game, is that you will improve much more quickly. In effect, you are doubling or tripling the amount of time you spend playing the game. Obviously, you need to know how to handle the equipment correctly before doing this. You do not want to reinforce bad habits. If you are familiar with the equipment and know how to use it correctly, you will make all the right moves when you practice in your imagination.

Visualization also allows you to prepare for situations you have yet to experience. Using mental imagery you can practice as often as you wish, so that when it is time to do it in real life you will be completely prepared and ready to succeed, because you have already done it many times in your mind.

Another benefit of visualization is that you can mentally practice difficult skills, and perfect your technique ahead of time. This also provides confidence in your ability to perform these difficult tasks in a competitive situation.

Creative visualization can also be used to eliminate negative thoughts and emotions. Nervousness, anxiety, stress, unrealistic expectations, and other pressures, such as the need to please others, have the potential to affect an athlete's chances of success.

Visualization is also helpful in motivating you to do everything that is required for success. If you find certain parts of your training boring, for instance, you can visualize yourself doing the less pleasant tasks with as much enthusiasm as the rest. This will help you put more energy into this part of your training program.

Many athletes find it helps them enormously to visualize themselves performing perfectly immediately before competing. Divers imagine themselves diving perfectly, skiers picture themselves making the best run possible, gymnasts see themselves doing a faultless routine, and team-sport athletes visualize themselves making key moves. These visualizations put them in the right frame of mind for success. They forget their fears and nervousness and focus on the achievement of their goals.

Likewise, many athletes like to relive their successful performances by visualizing them afterwards. This reinforces the feelings of success and helps them perform even better next time.

In your own rehearsal visualizations, see yourself playing the game or competing at your very best. You might like to slow the action down in your mind, so that you can visualize yourself in slow motion. Once you are certain that you are doing everything correctly, you can increase the speed.

During the actual performance you can use symbolic visualization. If you are competing in a running race, for instance, you might visualize someone whispering positive affirmations in your ear. You might picture someone pushing you on to success.

CHAPTER TWELVE

CAREER AND BUSINESS SUCCESS

"An entrepreneur is essentially a visualizer and an actualizer. He can visualize something, and when he visualizes it he sees exactly how to make it happen."

—ROBERT L. SCHWARTZ

According to the *Wall Street Journal*, most successful business executives visualize regularly and consider it one of the six most important activities they can do. "Top chief executives imagined every facet and feeling of what would have to happen to make a presentation a success, practicing a kind of purposeful daydreaming. A less effective executive would prepare his facts and agendas but not his psyche."[1] When Peter F. Drucker was asked to define leadership, he said,"Leadership is vision. There's nothing more to say."[2] Fred Smith (FedEx), Howard Schultz (Starbucks), Sam Walton (Walmart), Anita Roddick (Body Shop), and Michael Dell (Dell Computers) are just a few examples of successful, visionary entrepreneurs.

You can use the amazing power of creative visualization to help you progress at every stage of your career. You can use it to obtain a promotion, find a new and better position, start a business, or achieve any other business or professional goal.

Everyone knows that top athletes put in countless hours of training to achieve success. None of them relies on natural ability alone. Yet many people believe their natural abilities are all they need to rise up through the ranks in their business careers. It doesn't occur to them that they would rise higher, and faster, if they maintained a program of continual education and skill development. Creative visualization comes into this.

You have already learned how creative visualization can help you overcome personal problems and improve your personal life. There are a number of ways you can use creative visualization to help you progress in your business life.

Goal-setting plays an essential role in business life. A goal is basically a visualization of what you desire in the future. Some small businesses are run without goals, but you can guarantee that they will stay small until the management decide on some specific goals. You would never have heard of IBM, Microsoft, General Motors, or any other large corporation if they had not bothered to set goals. It is just as important to set goals for your own career, also.

Spend time working out short-term, medium-, and long-term goals for yourself. These should cover all areas of your life, not just your career. Set goals for your home and family life, further education, money, leisure, and spirituality.

Obviously, it is going to take a considerable amount of time for your long-term goals to be realized, and you may become discouraged. Fortunately, the success of your short- and medium-term goals will help keep you motivated. Keep visualizing all of your goals, no matter how long they take to manifest. Celebrate the achievement of every goal, no matter how small.

Obviously, it is hard to set goals if you are not sure what you want to achieve. Fortunately, creative visualization will help resolve this problem. Relax comfortably, and then visualize yourself one year from now. Notice your surroundings, possessions, hobbies, and interests. Spend as much time as you wish exploring your life twelve months from now. When you open your eyes, make notes about the experience. Determine if you would be happy living in the manner your visualization indicated.

A day or two later, repeat the visualization, but project yourself five years ahead. Question everything while enjoying the visualization. If your fortunes have dramatically improved, for instance, find out what you did or are doing to generate the extra money. Look at your career, home and family life, physical fitness, entertainment, and money. Again, take notes once you are done. Finally, project yourself ten years ahead, and repeat the process.

Once you have done this, you will be in a position to set goals to achieve the quality of life you desire one, five, and ten years from now. You may find that your projections for the future show a marked improvement in every area of your life. Now that you know how you accomplished it, you can set goals to speed up the process. If your projections showed you marking time, or even sliding backwards, you can set goals to help you create the type of life you desire. Repeat these visualizations of your future life until they reflect the sort of life you plan to enjoy.

You can also use creative visualization to help you in every other area of your working life.

Just recently I helped a young man who had to make a presentation to a group of senior executives in the corporation he worked in. Brad had never done anything like this before, and was understandably nervous. I taught him five visualization techniques that can be used in most types of business situations.

- PERFECT PERFORMANCE. I had Brad go through the entire meeting in his mind as frequently as possible before the event. In the visualization he saw himself confident and self-assured, giving a dynamic presentation to his superiors. He envisaged the entire scene, from the moment he arrived at work in the morning to the time he returned to his desk after receiving the congratulations of the people who had listened to him.

- MODELING. This technique is performed if you have a particular skill you want to develop. Think of someone who already possesses this skill. It doesn't matter who this person is. It might be a film star, a politician, or someone you know. Visualize yourself in a scene with this person, and watch them utilizing the quality you wish to develop. When you feel ready, switch roles with this person in your visualization. Picture yourself talking and acting in the same way that this person does. See yourself confidently using the skill that you wish to develop. Once you feel comfortable with this, visualize a situation at work and see yourself naturally using the quality you desire. This technique is great fun, as you can adopt skills from many different people. It is also extremely effective. Some years ago, I tried to help a salesman who was suffering from call reluctance. After receiving three or four "no's" in a row on the phone, he found it impossible to call the next person on his list. I taught him a number of techniques, none of which worked. However, the problem disappeared as soon as he started modeling himself on a colleague who immediately picked up the phone and dialed the next number no matter what responses he received. Brad used this modeling technique to gain the confidence he needed.

- SECRET ROOM. I have already mentioned this technique. In your visualizations you start by going to a secret, imaginary room where you can relax and resolve all the problems in your life. The main advantage of this technique is that after a bit of practice you will become totally relaxed as soon as you think of your special room. Once you have spent a bit of time relaxing in this room, you can take your visualization anywhere you wish. The other advantage of the secret room is that you can go there whenever you wish to eliminate fear, anxiety, stress, or pressures of any other sort. A few moments in your secret room are good for your physical body, as you will instantly relax as soon as you visualize it, but it also rejuvenates your mind and soul. Brad used this technique, along with the Perfect Performance technique, to prepare himself for his presentation.

- PREQUEL. This is a brief visualization of the Perfect Performance that is done immediately before the performance. You are likely to have seen many athletes do this before competing. I had Brad spend five to ten seconds immediately before his presentation seeing himself delivering his talk in exactly the way he wanted it to be.

- REVIEW. This is a visualization that is done after the event. Brad did this in the evening after his presentation. In a review visualization you look at every aspect of what actually happened, focusing on the positives, but also looking at the negatives to see how they could be eliminated next time. Every time you come across a negative, you need to mentally correct it so that you see yourself doing it successfully. Many people find it helpful to see the corrected version in slow motion, so they can sense everything that is going on. Once all the negatives have been turned around, the entire visualization can be watched again at normal speed. Finally, visualize all of the benefits that will accrue as a result of your performance. Some of these might be tangible, such as receiving a bonus or a signed order. However, do not forget the intangible benefits, such as knowing you performed well or the increased respect you receive from others.

I'm happy to report that Brad's presentation went well. He was not nervous because he had mentally rehearsed it many times in his mind beforehand. Consequently, he was able to concentrate on his delivery and message. Although there were no immediate tangible rewards, Brad was happy because he had made a good impression on the people who could help him progress in the company.

Brad is now using this technique in every part of his life. He was surprised to discover how useful it was to visualize important phone calls before making them. "I picture myself on the phone talking to the client," he told me. "I don't rehearse any conversation. I just visualize the feel of the call, and how positive and successful it is for everyone concerned. The amazing thing is that it obliterates any potential problems, because I always see the call going well."

It's not surprising that Brad's calls are so successful, as he has resolved them in his mind before making the call. An acquaintance of mine who sells real estate always visualizes herself showing people properties in her mind before doing it in reality. She spends ten to fifteen minutes doing this every morning before getting out of bed, and again at night before dropping off to sleep. Consequently, she has already answered people's objections in her mind, and can focus on showing them the properties that are right for them. She knows she is going to make the sale, because she has already been through the entire process in her mind. She stressed how important it was to do this consistently.

"Doing it once or twice, or even ten times, doesn't work," she told me. "You need to keep implanting that seed in your mind. Once you start doing it every day without fail, miracles start to happen."

A woman who used to come to my psychic-development classes uses creative visualization to come up with new business ideas. Every evening she looks at her business in different ways. She uses her imagination to come up with weird, wild, and wacky ideas—the stranger they are, the better. After the visualization session she writes them down and then evaluates them a day or two later.

"Some of these ideas are brilliant," she told me. "Others are simply crazy. But visualization enables me to experiment in my mind. In my imagination I can do anything at all, and there's no risk of harming my business." She laughed. "My kids say I have a wild imagination. I'd better add that these exercises help my concentration, too."

I was fascinated to hear her tell me of the process she uses, as she is one of the most creative people I have ever met. Creative visualization is an extremely effective tool for coming up with new ideas for your business or career.

You can also use creative visualization to further your career in other ways. One acquaintance of mine, a business consultant, teaches his clients how to visualize situations from the other person's point of view, as well as their own. Instead of visualizing a sales situation solely from the salesperson's point of view, he encourages them to visualize it from the prospect's viewpoint. This enables them to improve their presentations in ways that would never have occurred to them otherwise. It is an interesting exercise to mentally become your potential customer. It gives you an enormous business advantage to be able to see yourself through someone else's eyes. You will be amazed at what you "see" when you do this exercise.

Try doing this exercise before sending out a business letter. Visualize the recipient opening your letter and reading it. You'll be able to experience all the thoughts, feelings, and sensations that come into his or her mind. If nothing else, this exercise will improve your letter writing skills, as from now on, you'll probably decide to rewrite some of your letters before posting them.

This can be used in many other ways, as well. You might, for instance, temporarily become your partner, your son or daughter, your neighbor, someone who owes you money, and so on. The ability to visualize yourself from someone else's point of view is a valuable one that will enhance every aspect of your life.

An excellent salesman gave me a good suggestion recently. As well as using creative visualization for himself, he also paints pictures in his prospects' minds, so that they can see, feel, taste, and smell the offer he is presenting to them. In other words, he is getting them to see themselves using the product, or enjoying the benefits of owning it. Of course, once that stage is reached, the sale is almost guaranteed.

CHAPTER THIRTEEN

VISUALIZATION AND HEALTH

"A sound mind in a sound body; if the former be the glory of the latter, the latter is indispensable to the former."

—TRYON EDWARDS

Healers have used creative visualization as an aid to healing for thousands of years. People believed that evil spirits entered the body and caused illness, and visualizations were used to exorcise these negative entities from the patient. In ancient Egypt, followers of the god Hermes visualized themselves as fit and well. The ancient Greek healers instructed their patients to dream of being healed. Egyptian magician-priests used incantations that were a mixture of prayers and visualizations. Shamans performed healings by visualizing themselves undertaking a journey to find the sick person's soul, and then returning it. Even today, the Navaho Indians perform group visualizations to help their patients see themselves as healthy once again.[1]

In the 1920s, an American researcher named Edmund Jacobson was one of the first people to investigate the connection between the mind and the body. He discovered that when a volunteer visualized himself running, his leg muscles would start to twitch involuntarily.[2]

The medical profession has been interested in the potential healing power of visualization for at least fifty years.[3] The medical fraternity came to realize that stress can create a variety of health problems, such as high blood pressure, ulcers, and strokes. If our minds can cause bad health, surely we can also use our minds to create good health. Visualization is the perfect way of doing this.

Since 1965, Drs. Carl and Stephanie Simonton have helped numerous cancer patients visualize their bodies healing themselves. Dr. Simonton noticed that patients who had a positive attitude toward life were more likely to recover from their cancer than patients who were resigned or pessimistic. He also noticed that many terminal cancer patients lived long enough to participate in an event or celebration they had been looking forward to. Because he knew that the mind could influence people's immunological responses, he began devising experiments to help his patients develop a positive attitude toward life and toward healing their cancer.

Carl Simonton began by teaching his patients how to relax. Once in a suitably relaxed state, the patients are told to visualize a tranquil, peaceful scene. Then they visualize their cancer, and picture their immune systems working perfectly. After this, the patients visualize a wave of white blood cells swarming over the cancer, and taking away the malignant cells that have been killed or weakened by the radiation therapy. The white cells break down and dispose of all the malignant cells. At the end of this visualization the patients visualize themselves as being well and healthy once again.

The Simontons had some incredible successes with this technique. Unfortunately though, it did not work with everyone. Patients who believed in the technique, or were at least willing to suspend disbelief, received the best results. Without the element of belief, the visualization was simply a fantasy that had little or no effect.

Children proved extremely responsive to the Simonton technique, probably because they find it easier to use their imagination than adults. Consequently, many hospitals provide interactive video games in which their young patients can play at defeating their diseases.

Dr. Karen Olness of the Cleveland Children's Hospital gave a number of examples of children using visualization to heal and to control pain at a conference sponsored by the Institute of Noetic Sciences. One young hemophiliac visualized himself flying a plane through his blood vessels and releasing a load of Factor 8, the blood-clotting factor that his system lacked, whenever he needed to control bleeding.[4]

Garrett Porter was nine years old when he was diagnosed with an apparently inoperable brain tumor. He visualized a Star Wars-type battle, in which he led a space squadron who waged war against the tumor. The tumor disappeared within five months, with no need for any other therapy. Some years later, he and Pat Norris, his therapist, wrote a book about his experience called *Why Me? Learning to Harness the Healing Power of the Human Spirit.*[5]

However, visualizations involving killing a disease are not the right approach for everyone. The vast majority of people hate the thought of killing in any form. Consequently, they need a different approach, such as visualizing the disease melting or dissolving away. One commonly used method is to visualize the disease as a heap of brown sugar that steadily dissolves as warm water is poured onto it. Another possibility is to visualize the disease being sucked out of the body by a large vacuum cleaner. Obviously, the images do not have to be medically correct, just as long as the patient can clearly visualize them. In fact, there is some evidence that appears to indicate that visualizing in symbols is more effective than attempting to visualize the organs of the body. By focusing on a positive image, the patient calls on the body's natural defenses to fight the disease.

It is important to visualize the disease as weak and ineffectual, and the cure as strong and powerful. The illness might be seen as small, quivering with fear, and grey in color, for instance. To emphasize strength against weakness, some people like to visualize scenarios such as cops and robbers, or St. George and the dragon. At a talk I gave a few years ago, someone told me that she had visualized a large dog fighting a tiny dog. The tiny dog lay on its back and gave up. Her illness also gave up and disappeared.

There have been a number of instances in which the patient has had a spontaneous visualization that either explained the underlying cause of the illness or suggested a remedy. Jean Houston, a well-respected author, experienced this at the age of twenty-three. She was delirious with what her doctor said was influenza. Several ladies in flowered hats appeared in her imagination and told her that she should ask her mother to organize the blood test that is given to alcoholics. Her mother did, and the test showed that she was seriously ill with hepatitis.[6] Jean Houston experienced an involuntary visualization. It is also possible to perform a visualization of this sort deliberately, to uncover the origin of the disease, and to ask for assistance in curing it.

When she was five years old, Valere Althouse suffered a severe case of scarlet fever. She had a constant fever and her hair started to fall out. Eventually, she fell into a coma and was placed in the hospital. Although she was unconscious, she was aware of a doctor telling her parents there was nothing more they could do. Valere had never heard of visualization, but she immediately formed a picture in her mind of being fit and well again. As well as that, she wanted her hair back, but she wanted it to be curly, rather than straight as it had been before. The doctors were amazed that she survived, and surprised that she had suffered no brain damage as a result of the fever. Her hair started growing back, but it was curly, exactly as she had visualized.[7]

Visualization techniques can be used for any kind of illness, ranging from a sore throat to a life-threatening disease. In her book, *Why People Don't Heal and How They Can*, the well-known holistic healer, Caroline Myss, suggests that the patient imagine himself or herself in the center of a wheel surrounded by many spokes. Each spoke is labelled with a healing option, such as "prayer," "skilled physician," or "acupuncture." The patient visualizes the wheel spinning slowly, allowing the power and energy from each healing technique to flow into his or her body simultaneously as a complete, integrated whole.[8]

The power of the mind to heal has even been proved in a negative experiment. Dr. Thomas Holmes of Washington University conducted an experiment in which sample biopsies were taken from volunteers before and after certain subjects had been discussed. On speaking of the success of this project, Dr. Holmes said, "We caused tissue damage just by talking about a mother-in-law's coming to visit."[9]

This demonstrates the amazing power of the mind and the effect it has on the body. It puts a whole new perspective on the phrase "Physician, heal thyself." Obviously, if you are ill, you must obtain the best medical advice you can. However, you should also use creative visualization as often as possible, picturing yourself healthy and whole.

Healing a Minor Ailment

Creative visualization can be used to help relieve colds, influenza, bruising, cuts, and a variety of minor health problems.

Visualize in the usual manner, and then surround yourself with a pure, white light. Once you have done that, focus your attention on the particular problem you are concerned about. If it's a cut or a graze, for instance, focus your attention on this part of your body and visualize it bathed in a healing ointment or balm. Visualize the balm cleaning, healing, and restoring your body to full health. For something like influenza you might visualize the white light surrounding you gradually changing color into a vibrant, healing gold that permeates every cell of your body, restoring it to perfect health. You could use either of these methods for a cold. You might choose to use the first to help cure a sore throat, and the second for a cold that has progressed beyond that stage. You might use a mixture of both. What you choose to do is entirely up to you. The important thing is to clearly visualize healing energy going to the affected part of your body.

Before returning to everyday life, visualize some pleasant activities that you will be enjoying in the near future. Thank the universe for looking after you, and return to your day. Repeat as often as necessary, until you are restored to perfect health again.

Healthy Body Visualization

It is a good idea to regularly visualize yourself in perfect, vibrant health. To do this, visualize yourself surrounded by a pure, white light and affirm your good health. Visualize the pure, white light reaching into every cell of your body, filling you with energy and perfect health. Feel the perfect health inside you, and express a feeling of love to yourself. Visualize a few specific events in the future that you're looking forward to, and see yourself participating in them with enthusiasm, energy, and joy. Enjoy the healing, nurturing, white light for as long as you wish. When you feel ready, take a few slow, deep breaths and open your eyes. This is a good visualization to do when you're feeling tired or run-down, as it rejuvenates, restores, and nurtures every part of your body.

Controlling Stress

Stress is the effect that unpleasant events, real or imagined, have on the physical body. Stress seems to be an increasing problem for people worldwide. However, it has always been a fact of life. People living in prehistoric times must have suffered considerable stress in hunting for food and avoiding predators. Today the stress is caused by work, money, and family commitments. Lengthy commutes to and from work each day can be highly stressful. Some people are able to handle stress better than others, but everyone experiences it.

Stress over a period of time overloads the mind with negative thoughts. This causes self-doubt, lack of confidence, low self-esteem, and ultimately illness. Stress or tension headaches and back and neck pain are the most common examples of this. Prolonged stress can cause insomnia, ulcers, high blood pressure, heart attacks, and even asthma.

Fortunately, creative visualization can be used to reduce, and frequently eliminate, stress. Relax, and then visualize yourself in the most peaceful setting you can imagine. It makes no difference what setting you choose, just as long as it is peaceful and tranquil. Picture this scene using as many senses as possible.

Enjoy the peaceful scene for a minute or two, and then think of your need to eliminate the stress from your body. Visualize this stress in some sort of way. You might want to choose a color and a shape to represent your stress. Notice that you can make this colorful shape larger or smaller in your mind. Make it as small and ineffectual as possible while still keeping it visible.

Return to the peaceful scene, with your tiny shape of stress held between your thumb and first finger. Now you need to let this stress disappear. If there is a breeze in your scene, you might separate your fingers slightly and allow the stress to blow away. If you are relaxing beside a stream or river, you might place the stress on a small leaf or twig and allow the water to carry it out of sight. You might prefer to kick the stress up into the sky, or perhaps grind it to nothing beneath your feet. It makes no difference what you choose to do, just as long as you know the stress has completely disappeared.

Relax in your pleasant scene for as long as you wish. When you feel ready, return to your everyday life, feeling relaxed, invigorated, and free from stress.

If you are surrounded by constant stress, you should do this visualization at least once every day until the stress eases. If you suffer from occasional stress, you should do this visualization at the first sign that it is reappearing, and keep doing it regularly until life becomes smooth again.

Helping Others

You can use creative visualization to help heal others, also. It is important that, whenever possible, ask permission from the people you wish to help. They must be receptive to the idea, and must also want to be healed. Amazingly, not everyone wants healing. Some people get special attention or other benefits from their illness, and have no interest in becoming well again. These issues have to be dealt with before any healing can take place.

There may be times when you cannot wait to ask for permission. If someone is in a coma, for instance, you should start visualizing right away.

Start the visualization in the usual way. Sit down quietly, relax, and then visualize the person you wish to help. You will be able to mentally scan his or her body, and send healing to any areas of disease. Use your imagination and visualize the healing occurring. You may "see" the person receiving a miraculous, healing balm that draws out the illness. You may visualize small space ships attacking the disease. Rest assured that the right image will come into your mind.

Once you have finished the visualization, give thanks to the universe for allowing you to help in the healing process, and then come back to the present. Open your eyes and continue with your day, confident that the healing process is working. Do this every day, until the person regains his or her health. You can send loving thoughts to the person you are helping between the visualizations, but there is no need to dwell on the illness. You can rest assured that the universe will look after the matter for you, and you should carry on with your life in the usual way.

CHAPTER FOURTEEN

VISUALIZATION AND MAGIC

"Thought in the mind hath made us.
What we are by thought was wrought and built."

—JAMES ALLEN

Visualization is magical in the sense that it can be used to attract to you anything you desire. Fairy tales tell us that we can wish for something and it will somehow magically manifest. Of course, you now know that many other factors, apart from simply making a wish, are also involved. You need to be single-minded and focus your heart and mind on a specific goal. This is exactly what magicians do also.

Visualization plays an essential role in magic. Obviously, visualizing the successful result of a particular spell or rite makes the likelihood of success that much greater. In fact, there are magicians who use nothing but creative visualization to achieve their goals. However, most use creative visualization as part of the process, and accompany it with intent, energy, emotion, movement, ritual, and faith.

Visualization and Meditation

Visualization provides an effective method of quickly moving into a relaxed, meditative state. All you need is something to focus on. I enjoy gazing into the flame of a white candle.

To do this, sit down comfortably about six feet away from the object you are using. Gaze at the object, focusing on it without straining your eyes. Blink when necessary. When your eyes feel tired, allow them to close, but continue to visualize whatever it is you are focusing on. If the mental image fades, open your eyes for a few seconds to refresh your mind. As well as leading you into a relaxed, meditative state, this exercise helps you develop your visualization skills.

Continue to visualize the object for as long as you wish. When you feel ready, allow the image to fade until it disappears completely. At this point you could either clear your mind entirely, and enjoy the meditation, or you might prefer to see what images come to you from your subconscious mind. Enjoy being in the meditative state for a while before returning to your everyday life.

Pathworking

Many rituals include a guided visualization that takes the participants on an imaginary, vividly realized journey that is intended to bring insight, wisdom, or a relevant message. This visualization is often known as a "pathworking." When performed in a group, one person directs the proceedings. He or she helps the participants to relax completely, and then takes them on an imaginary journey that enables them to access the latent power that resides deep within. This gives them the insight and power they need to achieve their aims. This powerful force is multiplied when created by a group, and creates a strong emotional experience that helps the participants to achieve their goals.

Pathworking also stimulates the brow (or third eye), chakra, allowing feelings and intuitions to flow freely.

Here is an example of a pathworking:

- Relax completely.

- Visualize yourself in a pleasant outdoor scene. You feel comfortable, warm, and curious about some aspect of your life. You become aware of all the sights, sounds, smells, and feelings of this pleasant environment.

- You notice a small path leading to a grove of trees on a small hill. You decide to follow the path to see where it leads.

- You enter the grove of trees. It is slightly cooler here, but you still feel comfortable. You notice a sense of excitement, and start walking with greater purpose than before.

- You reach the top of the hill where you find a quaint-looking cottage with a brightly colored front door. You knock on the door.

- After a brief wait, the door opens and you gaze in amazement at the person facing you. This person hands you something that enables you to understand what is going on in your life.

- You express your appreciation and gratitude, and then return through the grove of trees and along the path, back to where you started.

- When you feel ready, open your eyes and think about the imaginary journey you have just undertaken, and the knowledge and insight you have gained. The person (or animal) who opened the door will have relevance in your life. It is worth spending time thinking about why that particular person (or animal) appeared in your visualization, as it will usually be a surprise. If it is an animal, think about the symbolism that this animal creates in your mind. A deer might engender feelings of gentleness or speed, for instance, while a lion might make you think of strength, power, and nobility. Maybe you would benefit by working with the energies of that particular animal. Think also about whatever it was you were given, as it will have relevance, too.

It is always best to finish the pathworking at the place you began. This creates a definite start and end to the experience.

You can use pathworking for a variety of purposes. You might use it to gain protection, for instance. To achieve this, pay a visit to a safe, secure place where nothing can harm you. If you require courage, go on an expedition to find someone who will give you the strength and courage that you require. You might explore different myths and legends, taking on the role of one of the characters. You will gain additional insight by repeating the pathworking as each of the main characters in turn. You might choose to go back and forth through time to different places where you can learn the lessons you need to make the most of this incarnation. Pathworking is a useful tool, but it should never be used as an amusement. If you determine what you want to achieve before embarking on any pathworking, you will make the most out of the experience.

Contacting Your Guardian Angel

You can use creative visualization to contact your guardian angel. Doing this allows you access to your subconscious mind, which knows everything.

Close your eyes and relax. Visualize yourself in your secret room, or in a safe place where you feel totally relaxed and comfortable. Tell yourself that you want to meet your guardian angel. If you are in your secret room, turn to face the entrance. If you are outdoors, look in the direction where you think your angel will appear.

Be patient, and wait for your guardian angel to appear. If you are visualizing an outdoor scene, you might first see your guardian angel as a speck in the distance. You will gradually notice more and more details as your guardian angel gets closer. If you are visualizing your secret room, your guardian angel might open the door and walk in, or may suddenly appear in front of you.

You might be surprised at your guardian angel. Your angel might be taller or shorter than you imagined. The clothing, hair, and features might not be what you expected. Your angel may, or may not, have visible wings.

Start by asking this angel if he or she is, in fact, your guardian angel. If it is not, send the angel away, telling it to send you your guardian angel. You are omnipotent in a creative visualization. If the figure that appears seems aggressive or threatening, you can immediately send it away.

Once you have met your guardian angel, you might choose to take a walk together, or you may sit down for a chat. If you are in your secret room, take your guardian angel for a brief tour. Ask your guardian angel any questions you wish. When you have finished, say goodbye. Hug or kiss your guardian angel if it seems appropriate. Tell your angel that you will be calling on him or her regularly from now on. Also suggest that your guardian angel visit you whenever it seems appropriate.

Repeat this exercise in a day or two. Once you have become used to your guardian angel's presence, visualize a number of different settings in which to meet. You want your guardian angel to come to you whenever necessary, not just when you're in your secret place.

Your guardian angel can also accompany you when you are pathworking. This is particularly useful when your life seems confusing or difficult.

At one time I lived close to Hampton Court, in England, and frequently visited the maze in the gardens. If I have a difficult decision to make, I meet my guardian angel at the entrance to the maze. Usually, the matter has been resolved by the time we emerge again.

Obviously, you can use the same techniques to contact any type of guide. I use my guardian angel because I have a strong interest in the subject of angels. You may prefer a totally different type of guide. It makes no difference if this person ever lived, is imaginary, or is even an animal. Someone I know calls on his deceased grandfather when he needs help and advice. You may choose to visualize a wizard, witch, priest, priestess, god, or goddess. You might choose to visualize a friendly animal. One person might choose a lion, for symbolic reasons. Another person might be fearful of lions and choose a gentler animal, such as a deer or a rabbit. You might not deliberately choose a certain person or animal. If you need help or advice, ask for guidance, and see what comes to your aid. It might even be an imaginary animal, as anything is possible in a visualization.

Always ask the person who comes if he or she is your guide. Ultimately, it makes no difference what form your guide appears in, as he or she will have access to your sub-conscious mind and be able to give you good advice.

You are not restricted to one guide, either. You may choose to have different guides for different purposes. One may help you further your career, another might assist you with close relationships, while another might help you re-decorate your home.

Your guides can be of either sex, and it is common for people to have both male and female guides, as we all have masculine and feminine sides to our makeup. Your guides may also vary in age. It might seem surprising to have a young child as a guide, for instance, but the choice will be appropriate, as there is at least a trace of the child you used to be still inside you.

Symbols

In magic, different symbols are frequently used as focal points to help develop visualization skills. The five Hindu Tattva symbols of elemental power are good examples. They represent the five elements of:

Earth–Yellow Square

Water–Blue Circle

Fire–Red Equilateral Triangle (pointing upwards)

Air–Silver Crescent (lying on its back)

Ether–Purple Egg

(Some people in the West use the crescent to represent Water, and the circle to represent Air. This is because the crescent is similar to the Moon, and consequently can represent lunar energy, which relates to the Water element. Also, Air appears to be blue when you look at the sky, making a blue circle an appropriate symbol. For the purposes of these exercises, I have retained the original Indian associations.)

You might find it helpful to make up a set of Tattva symbols to help you when you first start working with them. Display the Earth symbol (yellow square) in a position where you can look at it comfortably without raising or lowering your head. You should sit about six feet away from it. Relax as much as possible while looking at the symbol. Gaze steadily at it for as long as you can. Allow your eyes to close as soon as they start to feel heavy. See how long you can hold the image of the yellow square in your mind without distorting or changing it in any way. If it starts to change color, size, or shape, open your eyes to see what the symbol looks like, and repeat the exercise.

The goal is to be able to visualize the symbol in your mind for ten minutes without losing concentration. Once you can do this, repeat the exercise with each of the other symbols. You are likely to find this exercise hard to do at first, as your mind is likely to wander. However, if you practice this exercise every day, you will soon find that you can focus on the symbol for ten minutes with ease.

Once you can clearly visualize all five symbols in your mind, you will be able to use this skill to create magic in your life. Think about something that would improve your life in some way. Think of this desire in terms of symbols.

Create a shape for your request, and then give it a color. Most of the time, the design and color will spring to your mind as soon as you decide to create a symbol. However, there will be times when you need to think about the necessary symbol for a while before it comes to you.

Once you have the required symbol, sit down and relax in the same way you did with the Tattva symbols. You may find it helpful to draw the symbol first, so that you can focus on it. However, the practice you have put in with the Tattva symbols will probably enable you to close your eyes and clearly visualize any symbol. I like to draw the symbol, as I can hang it on a wall to act as a silent affirmation. Whenever I happen to see it, I am reminded of my request to the universe.

To create magic, you need to focus on your chosen symbol. Imagine yourself already in possession of whatever it is you are seeking, and then give it as much emotional charge as you possibly can. Visualize your symbol pulsating with energy as it absorbs all the emotion you can give it. Once you have done that, fill the symbol with the power of your will, your absolute desire to possess whatever it is you are seeking. When your symbol seems ready to explode with the power of your drive, energy, intent, focus, belief, emotion, and will, consciously send it out to the universe where it will manifest your desire. I visualize this as an enormous current of energy that sends the symbol shooting out into the universe. Once you have done this, give thanks to the universe, and carry on with your day, absolutely convinced that your desire will manifest itself in your life.

Tarot Cards

Tarot cards are extremely useful for visualization purposes, as they contain a wealth of images and symbolism. Some of these are easier to identify than others.

The Strength card, for instance, is an easy one. This card depicts a young woman with her hands around the muzzle of a lion. This card symbolizes strength, fortitude, determination, endurance, and courage. It also symbolizes the necessary strength of character to follow the right path, no matter what the cost. If you need strength to achieve your goals, you could sit down and gaze at the Strength card. Observe it closely. When you feel ready, close your eyes and see if you can clearly visualize the card in your mind. Once you can do this, mentally place yourself inside the card, and see what comes to you. Allow the strength of the card to fill you to overflowing with its energy, and then project yourself forward to a situation in which you will require strength. Watch yourself handling the situation from a position of strength. See yourself being fair to everyone involved, and remaining calm, relaxed, and centered, no matter what occurs. See yourself, after the incident is over, feeling pleased and happy with the outcome.

You can find any quality you wish in the tarot deck. If you desire a close and fulfilling relationship, for instance, you might meditate and then visualize the Two of Cups. If you wish to progress in your career, the Seven of Pentacles might be a good choice. If you seek a way out of a stressful situation, you might visualize the Four of Swords. The Six of Wands might be a useful card to meditate on and visualize when you are making progress but wish to move further or faster. It is a card that promises success as a direct result of your skills and talents.

Even the cards that people consider to be negative can be useful in certain situations. If you have an addictive personality, for instance, you may find that meditating on and then visualizing the Devil card will give you insights into why you abuse certain substances.

If a stage in your life has come to an end, for any reason, you may find that visualizing the Death card will enable you to see that the ending of something also marks a new beginning. This can help you let go of things that you have been hanging onto, to make way for the new.

Your knowledge of visualization will be useful if you are learning how to use the tarot, or any other divination system. You can visualize each card in turn, and see what insights occur to you. It can be helpful to enter the minds of the people depicted in the cards and see what they have to tell you.

Instant Visualization

Magicians also use creative visualization for a variety of other purposes. If they find themselves in a potentially difficult or stressful situation, they immediately visualize themselves inside a large bubble of protection. If they feel ill, they visualize themselves surrounded with healing energy. If they want to strengthen their aura, they visualize it growing in energy and power. If they need more personal power for any purpose, they visualize themselves as being filled to overflowing with unlimited power and energy.

Most practitioners of Wicca erect a physical magic circle to create a sacred space that they can work within. However, some simply visualize the circle and use that, finding it just as effective as a physical circle.

CHAPTER FIFTEEN

25 WAYS TO ENHANCE YOUR LIFE WITH CREATIVE VISUALIZATION

*"Every man should frame life that at some future hour
fact and his dreamings meet."*

—Victor Hugo

As you have already seen, creative visualization can be used in many different ways. People have used it to create business empires, and to win gold medals at the Olympics. A common complaint I hear is that these people are exceptional and would have achieved their goals with or without creative visualization. It is impossible to answer this, as some people appear to be driven to success by some force inside them. Most people, (fortunately, I think) lack this constant drive to achieve huge goals. However, many people who achieve extraordinary goals are not driven. They have set worthwhile goals for themselves, and then set out to achieve them. To help them do this, they use every tool that they can find, and creative visualization is potentially one of the most useful.

However, creative visualization is not solely for huge goals. It can be used to achieve any goal or desire. No matter how humble or lofty your goals may be, creative visualization will help you achieve them. Here are 25 different ways that you can use creative visualization to enhance your life.

Developing Skills

Not long ago, I had a puncture and had to change a tire on my car. It took me about fifteen minutes. Shortly after that, I took my car in for a service and saw a young mechanic changing a tire. It took him three or four minutes to perform a task that had taken me five times as long. Admittedly, he was doing it in a garage, with plenty of tools to choose from, but all the same, he performed the task more efficiently and in a much shorter period of time than I did, because he had developed specialist skills. Where I had fumbled and cursed, he was able to get on with the job because he had performed it hundreds of times before and knew exactly what to do.

Steve Backley, the champion British javelin thrower, took part in an experiment at Loughborough University. Three groups were given ten minutes to assemble 32 bolts, nuts, and washers. Beforehand, one group was given ten minutes to practice assembling them. The second group spent ten minutes visualizing the task, and the third group did nothing at all. When the experiment took place, the first group assembled all thirty-two sets, the second group put together thirty, while the third group assembled only twenty-two.[1] This experiment clearly shows that you can develop your skills at anything by spending time visualizing the process. The visualizers in this experiment did almost as well as the people who had practiced, and both of these groups were well ahead of the group that had done neither.

Affirmations to help the process include, "I am talented, skilled and competent" and "I constantly develop my skills."

Developing Talents

You can use visualization to develop your skills at virtually anything. I am hopelessly impractical, but have learned how to do many household tasks out of necessity. As a result, I have used creative visualization to develop a degree of skill in these areas. If it is possible to use visualization to develop your skills at something you are not naturally good at, imagine the incredible progress you could make if you used visualization to help develop a talent.

In Chapter Eleven, we learned how successful athletes use creative visualization to develop their talent at different sports. The same methods can be used to develop any other talent.

Way back in 1915, Edwin Hughes taught pianists to visualize themselves playing the pieces they were learning. "They must set aside some time daily for practice away from the instrument," he wrote, "be it during the afternoon walk or a quiet hour with closed eyes in the armchair, and must be able to mentally go through the compositions studied with as little hesitation as when seated before the instrument. Every opportunity would in fact be taken for this mental practice, for the pianist who plays in public must live with his pieces constantly. He must know them, and not simply remember them. They must be a very part of him."[2]

The late Glenn Gould was one of the greatest pianists of the twentieth century. He had a reputation for playing even the most difficult works effortlessly. He did this by closing his eyes, and imagining that he was across the room watching himself play. By visualizing himself playing the piece perfectly in his mind, he was able to play it the same way in real life.[3]

This works for any talent, not just playing the piano. If you have a talent of any sort, you will be able to develop it more quickly, and take it much, much further if you use creative visualization techniques.

Suggested affirmations to help the process include, "I am creative, talented, and inspired" and "My talent at (whatever it happens to be) is improving all the time."

Enhancing Creativity

Everybody is creative. Every time you have a thought you are creating something. All ideas start in the imagination. Creative visualization makes use of your imagination to create whatever it is you want in your life. Consequently, creative visualization is an extremely useful and practical way to enhance your creativity.

Albert Einstein wrote that he discovered the theory of relativity when he visualized himself riding on a ray of light. Henry Moore, the British sculptor, wrote that a sculptor "mentally visualizes a complex form *from all round itself*: he knows while he looks at one side what the other side is like; he identifies himself with its center of gravity, its mass, its weight; he realizes its volume as the space that the shape displaces in the air."[4]

Highly creative people visualize automatically. However, it can be done consciously as well. In the 1960s, Dr. Alex Osborn developed a technique called applied imagination. The basis of his idea was to let the imagination roam freely and to come up with as many ideas as possible, without pausing to evaluate any of them. Once this has been done, the ideas are looked at again, and carefully evaluated and considered.[5] Temporarily suspending judgment dramatically increases the number of ideas that come to your mind.

An effective approach when using creative visualization to enhance your creativity is to maintain an attitude of positive expectancy. Relax, and let your mind roam freely, confident that it will come up with many solutions, at least one of which will be exactly what you desire. Allow the different ideas and images to come and go without any conscious interference. There is no need to worry that you will not remember everything that occurs, as you will have total recall afterwards. When you feel ready, take a deep breath and mentally count to five. Open your eyes, and enjoy the feelings of enthusiasm and excitement that will come into your mind. When you feel ready, evaluate all the ideas that came to you during the visualization.

You may not receive the result you desire on the first visualization. Frequently, creative ideas need an incubation period before appearing in your mind. This is why many good ideas come when you least expect them. Pablo Picasso was well aware of the importance of the incubation period. In the film *The Mystery of Picasso*, he said, "It would be very interesting to record photographically—not the stages of a painting—but its metamorphoses. One would see perhaps by what course a mind finds its way toward the crystallization of its dream."[6]

Regular use of affirmations will enhance the creative process. "Creative ideas come to me all the time" and "I experience amazing insights every day" are examples.

Dealing with Your Difficult People

Many years ago, I spent a few months working in a warehouse. The work itself was boring, but what made the job particularly unpleasant was the woman who ran the office. I have no idea what was going on in her life, but she derived great pleasure from being as rude and unhelpful as she possibly could to the people she considered beneath her, which was everyone in the warehouse. I was taken aback, as I had not encountered such rudeness before. Every day, at morning and afternoon tea, the rest of the warehouse staff thought up ways to annoy her, as they wanted to get even. As far as I know, none of these ideas ever got past the suggestion stage, but I thought it would be interesting to try to get on with her.

Before going to sleep at night, I visualized myself at work in the warehouse on the following day. I pictured this woman greeting me with a smile on her face. I imagined having conversations with her, and even saw us both laughing at a joke.

I did this for a whole week before anything happened. One morning, shortly before morning tea, she called me into her office and said she'd been watching me, and was impressed with my work. As a result, she was putting me in charge of one of the sections of the warehouse. This unpaid promotion meant nothing to me, as I was not planning to stay, but I was excited that my visualizations were starting to bear fruit. I kept on with the visualizing, and after about another week, she started coming into the warehouse, purely to have a conversation with me. Before long, we were even sharing jokes.

I had another similar experience with a woman at my local post office. She didn't appear to enjoy dealing with the public, and was always grouchy and brusque with the customers. I decided that I would get her to smile. I began by being particularly pleasant to her. That had no effect whatsoever. I sent her a Christmas card, care of the post office, thinking that a postal employee might enjoy receiving a card. It was ignored. Finally, I began visualizing myself walking into the post office. There was the usual line of people there. This woman would look up from serving a customer, see me, and greet me with a smile.

I told a few people what I was doing, and they all told me it was a complete waste of time. The woman enjoyed being miserable, and I would not live long enough to see her smile. I'm happy to say they were wrong. My visualization eventually worked. After two years of my visualizing her smile, she greeted me warmly one day. We now enjoy brief, cordial conversations every time I go to the post office. I have yet to see her smile at anyone else, but I am rewarded with one every time I go in.

I have found visualizing a positive outcome to be extremely helpful when dealing with difficult people. Like most people, my initial reaction when faced with rudeness or unpleasantness is to give as good as I get. However, that helps no one, and I have learned that a bit of kindness and understanding, coupled with visualization, works much better. Try it yourself, next time you have to deal with a difficult person and see how much more pleasant the situation becomes.

Affirmations that will help in these situations include, "I am calm and in control in every type of situation" and "I constantly express my love to everyone."

Dealing with Your Boss

I think I'm an easy person to get along with, but on two occasions in my life I have told a boss exactly where to go. In both cases I then resigned. In these tougher economic times, this is not the best way to handle difficult bosses.

A much more preferable solution is to visualize you and your boss in a situation that you might have found difficult in the past. Visualize yourself handling it with effortless ease. Imagine your boss commending you for your hard work and initiative. Visualize as many different types of scenarios as possible. You may like to replay some difficult scenes from the past, but in your re-enactment, see them replayed in the way you would have liked them to be.

You will experience a number of benefits from these visualizations. You are likely to see your boss in a different way, and gain an understanding of the problems he or she faces. Your approach to your boss will change, and this will create a more harmonious work environment.

Suggested visualizations include, "I can see other people's points of view as well as my own" and "I understand and get along with everyone."

Dealing with Difficult Situations from the Past

Everyone has memories of embarrassing or badly handled situations. As there is nothing you can do about the situation now, it is a waste of time to constantly berate yourself about them. Thoughts along the lines of "How could I have been so stupid?" do no good, and effectively become negative visualizations. Fortunately, we can use creative visualization to eliminate these problems.

Relax, and relive the negative experience in your mind. Try to see the scene in as detached a manner as possible. By doing this, you may gain insights as to why you behaved in the way you did. You might, for instance, realize that you were only four years old at the time, and your behavior, although not good, was probably a sensible way of dealing with it for someone that age.

Let go of the scene in your mind, and create an imaginary scene in which you are talking to someone who was also involved in the situation. Apologize to that person, and listen to what they have to say in return. Repeat with everyone who was involved. Finally, visualize the situation again, and firmly say goodbye to it. It now belongs only to the past. You have done all that you can to resolve the situation, and you need not carry it any longer. Take three deep breaths, and open your eyes. Repeat this exercise as many times as necessary until you find that you are no longer dwelling on it.

Suggested affirmations are, "I let go of the past" and "I live in the present and make the most of every day."

Dealing with Difficult Situations in the Future

We are inclined to make matters worse in our imaginations than they ever are in real life. If you are aware of a difficult situation coming up in the near future, you can use creative visualization to remove any worry or fears you might have about the object or situation.

Relax and think about the upcoming event. Determine the level of anxiety you feel on a scale from one to ten. Once you have thought of a number, think about a safe, relaxing, peaceful, and pleasant scene from your past. Visualize the upcoming event again, but this time see yourself handling the situation in a calm, confident manner. Again determine the level of anxiety you feel. Continue switching from the peaceful scene to the one that is causing worry, until you feel no appreciable anxiety in your mind or body. Continue to regularly visualize yourself handling the situation in the way you would like to until the event has occurred.

Suggested affirmations include, "I live in the present," "My future is bright," and "I have all the strength necessary to handle every type of situation."

Handling a Proposed Change

Most people hate change. They would prefer to continue doing what they have always done rather than take a risk that might increase the quality of their lives. The fact that you have bought this book shows that you want to improve your life and are not crippled by the prospect of change. However, there will be times when you're not sure whether or not to decide on a difficult issue. Fortunately, there is a creative visualization technique called double imagery[7] that can help you evaluate change, and make good choices.

Relax, and visualize your life in the near future if you do not make the proposed change. Once you have clearly visualized this, let it go, and then visualize your future as it would be after you had made the change. Clearly sense the benefits of making the change. Become aware of any possible disadvantages, also. Return to the first scenario, and see the advantages and disadvantages of not making the change. Switch between the two scenes several times to clarify both scenarios in your mind. Finally, visualize yourself in a safe, comfortable place evaluating the advantages and disadvantages of both possibilities. You might like to see yourself writing down a list of the pros and cons of each choice. Once you have made a decision, return to the scenario that you prefer and visualize it again. Do the same with the other scenario, and then return to the one you have picked. Ask yourself if you are making the right decision, and see how your body reacts. When you feel ready, open your eyes. If this exercise fails to clarify the situation to your satisfaction, continue doing it until one of the two possibilities totally overwhelms the other.

Of course, from time to time you'll be faced with changes that you must accept, no matter what your own desires are. In these cases, look at both scenarios in the same way as before, but focus on the benefits of making the change, and the disadvantages of refusing to accept it.

Suggested affirmations include, "I welcome change" and "Life holds unlimited opportunities for me."

Achieving Desirable Outcomes

You can use creative visualization for any type of situation that has a number of possible solutions. Determine the outcome that you feel will be most beneficial for everyone concerned, and rehearse the resolution in your creative visualizations as many times as possible ahead of time.

Suggested affirmations include, "I enjoy discovering positive outcomes" and "I desire success for everyone."

An elderly man I met at a workshop told me how he had used visualization to maintain contact with his two grandsons. For years he had looked after them every Saturday. Sometimes they went to his home, where he taught them carpentry. At other times he'd take them to the movies or a game. He was retired, and spent every week looking forward to Saturday. His grandsons did too.

This routine carried on after his son's marriage broke up and his son left the home. The boys and their mother struggled financially after this, and the grandfather helped by buying groceries and clothes for them every now and again. One day, the mother told him that she was hard up, and if he wanted to keep seeing his grandsons, he would have to pay her $100 every time he visited. The old man could not afford to do this.

"Talk to your son then," she said. "Get him to send more money."

He called his son and listened to his tale of woe.

"She's robbing me blind as it is," he was told. "She's not getting a cent more out of me."

When he arrived to pick up his grandsons the following Saturday, his daughter-in-law asked for the money. As he did not have it, she turned him away. He tried again the following week, with the same result. He heard his grandsons pleading with her, but her mind was made up.

The old man resented his daughter-in-law for using the boys in this way, but was able to see the situation from her point of view. He pondered the matter for several days. He rejected the idea of pleading with his son. He could sell or borrow against his home, but that didn't seem sensible at his age. Even negotiating a smaller figure with his daughter-in-law would result in bitterness.

He realized his daughter-in-law's decision punished everyone involved. The man and his grandsons missed spending time with each other, while the boys' mother missed out on a day free of parental responsibilities.

The old man constantly visualized happy Saturdays with his grandsons. He saw himself enjoying a pleasant conversation with their mother when he picked them up. He even visualized himself phoning his son to tell him how much fun they were having. He was careful not to attach any bitterness or blame on anyone. He believed this was the best possible outcome for everyone concerned. For weeks he visualized each moment of a perfect Saturday.

Finally, after four weeks, his daughter-in-law phoned. She had found a part-time job in a department store. Would he be willing to look after the boys every Saturday?

"The only thing I didn't visualize was her getting a part-time job," he told me. "Yet it made perfect sense. She loves it, and it gives her the extra money she needs. We went through a miserable time, but it worked out well in the end."

Handling Irrational Fears

Not long ago, a middle-aged man came to see me. His marriage had ended a few years earlier, and he wanted to start dating again. However, he had developed a phobia about asking anyone out. Meeting women was not a problem, as he dealt with many of them in the course of his work. However, he became paralyzed with fear at the thought of asking one out. He knew this fear was irrational, but all the same it was having a dramatic effect on his life. I taught him a simple, humorous exercise that eliminated the problem in a matter of minutes.

I had him relax and, in his imagination, see himself asking a woman for a date and getting turned down.

"How do you feel?" I asked him.

"Pretty stupid," he replied.

"Okay, you feel stupid. So what? Is it the end of the world?"

He sighed. "I guess not, but I don't like feeling stupid."

"Are you a good, honest, caring person?" I asked.

"Yes."

"In that case, who's the stupid one, you or her?"

"Me, 'cause I got turned down."

"And because of that, you'll never ask another woman out? That is stupid."

There was a long silence. "I guess it is," he said at last.

"Good. Now approach another woman and ask her out. What does she say?"

"Something rude."

"How do you feel?"

"Stupid."

"Uh huh. So every time you get turned down you feel stupid. Now imagine yourself with a gorgeous woman, and you're deeply in love. How many times would it be worth feeling stupid to get to that state? Once, twice, a hundred times?"

He laughed at that, and I knew the problem was resolved. Shortly after that, after only a couple of rejections, he found an attractive woman to share his life with.

The secret to this technique is to imagine a worst-case scenario, and see if you can handle it. In your mind you can make it as far-fetched and ridiculous as you wish. In reality, the problem will never be as bad as the worst-case situation. Knowing that you can handle that makes it a simple matter to overcome the irrational fear.

Suggested affirmations include, "Everything goes well for me today, and every day" and "I am confident and in control of my mind and emotions."

Controlling Eating Habits

The whole Western world seems to be fighting a battle against obesity. Every second person seems to be on a diet, even though the success rates of diets are unbelievably low. Obviously, you need to eat for nutrition and health, but food is so plentiful that the temptation to overeat, or to binge on inappropriate food, is constantly present. Fortunately, you can use creative visualization to help you reach and maintain the ideal weight for you.

In your visualization, ask your guardian angel to join you (see Chapter Fourteen). Ask him or her why you overeat. The answer may be that you are lonely, bored, or stressed. Perhaps you eat for comfort, somehow nurturing yourself by eating too much of the wrong foods. Maybe you overeat to punish yourself. The answers you receive may not be what you expect. Ask any other questions that seem relevant. Maybe you've joined a gym but seldom have a workout. Ask your guardian angel why you subconsciously resist exercising. Maybe you crave certain types of food. Your angel will explain why you do this.

Once you have all the answers you need, devise some affirmations to help you change your eating habits. Visualize yourself at least once every day, the size, shape, and weight that you desire. Whenever possible, do your visualizations immediately before eating, and see yourself eating slowly, enjoying smaller portions than before, but feeling completely satisfied after every meal. Remain confident that you will reach your goal.

Obviously, the length of time required depends on the amount of weight you want to lose. Patience is definitely required, as rapid-weight-loss methods never work for long. You can lose a few pounds in a matter of weeks, but you should allow at least a year for major weight loss. Keep on top of your thinking. Use positive affirmations and celebrate all of your successes along the road to becoming the new you.

Your guardian angel will help you to gradually change your approach to food and exercise. Have regular sessions with him or her. Determine to eat enough good quality, nutritious food for your body's needs and then stop. Establish an exercise program that you enjoy. Continue with your daily visualizations and know, without any doubt, that you will reach your goal.

Suggested affirmations include, "I love my body and enjoy taking care of it" and "I enjoy eating the correct amount of good, healthy food."

Stopping Smoking

There are three factors involved with smoking. There is the addiction, of course. Nicotine is an extremely addictive drug. Fortunately, it leaves your body within 72 hours. The psychological factors involved with smoking are more important than the addiction. It can give you something to do with your hands, make you feel more confident, or even provide a slow method of killing yourself. The most important factor of all is the smoking habit. People often light a cigarette when they're on the phone, in the car, or enjoying a drink. Frequently, they don't even realize what they're doing—the lit cigarette somehow appears in the hand.

Every smoker knows that it is a filthy, expensive, and potentially fatal practice. Unfortunately, because it is a complex mixture of addiction, psychological reasons, and habit, many smokers find it hard to quit. They may also fear the withdrawal stage, or the possibility of gaining weight.

If you want to quit, visualize your guardian angel and ask for the reasons why you smoke. Find out what benefits you gain from the habit. Think about these once you have finished the visualization, and decide if the time is right to give up nicotine. Visualize again the next day, and have a look at your future, free of nicotine. See how your body reacts to this prospect.

Once you have done this, set a date for quitting, ideally two or three days ahead. This gives you time to think about your reasons for quitting. It also gives you time to create some positive affirmations. You might say to yourself, "I'm a healthy non-smoker;" or "I choose not to smoke. I'm in control, and am a permanent non-smoker."

On the day you choose to quit, clean all the ashtrays in your home and put them away. Sit down comfortably and relax. Visualize yourself as a fit, healthy, vibrant, permanent non-smoker. Go through all your reasons for wanting to quit, and congratulate yourself for doing something extremely worthwhile for you and your loved ones. Take yourself through a normal day, and see yourself doing all the things you normally do, but now you are doing them as a non-smoker. Congratulate yourself on the decision you have made. Feel proud and positive. It's a major accomplishment, and you should allow yourself to feel proud.

Repeat the visualization at least once a day for ten days. If you have a desire for a cigarette, give yourself a five- or ten-second visualization to cement in the pride and accomplishment of what you are doing. You enjoy becoming and remaining a permanent non-smoker. After a few days, you'll be able to change the visualization to one of congratulating yourself for becoming a permanent non-smoker.

After a month or so, do something to reward yourself. You have accomplished something remarkable and deserve a celebration. If, at any time in the future you have an urge for a cigarette, repeat the visualization until the desire disappears.

Suggested affirmations include, "I am proud to be a non-smoker" and "My desire for good health is much stronger than my desire for a cigarette."

Curing Insomnia

Insomnia is a common problem. Fortunately, it is one that can usually be helped by creative visualization. The exceptions is if the insomnia is caused by a dependence on drugs or alcohol. You will need medical help if these are the cause of your insomnia. Tea, coffee, and soda can also affect your sleep. If you have problems getting to sleep, you should stop using these stimulants as early in the day as possible.

Another problem some people have is that they start worrying as soon as they get to bed. If you are inclined to worry once you turn the light out, tell yourself firmly that you'll do all your worrying at eleven o'clock the next morning, and that you do not need to concern yourself with it now.

One big advantage creative visualization has in curing insomnia is that the process involves total relaxation. When most people go to bed at night, once they are relaxed, they fall asleep. This is what will happen when you lie down in bed and perform a visualization to help you fall asleep.

Once you are relaxed, go to your secret place. Make yourself as comfortable as possible, and look around. If you are in your secret room, you can look at the beautiful objects you have inside the room. You might turn on some pleasant music, and lie down in a luxurious bed, feeling warm, comfortable, safe, and very, very tired. If you are outdoors, you can admire the view for a while, and then lie down and close your eyes, enjoying the pleasant warmth of the day, and allowing it to make you feel more and more drowsy.

If this does not make you fall asleep, think about something pleasant that you experienced recently. Enjoy reliving the experience, and then go back to an earlier pleasant time. Keep doing this until you fall asleep.

Suggested affirmations include, "I enjoy relaxing and sleeping in bed" and "When I go to bed, I relax and fall asleep quickly."

Dealing with Difficult Emotions

Even positive emotions can be hard to handle. Consequently, it's not surprising that many people fight a constant battle with negative emotions, such as anger, fear, and guilt. A relative of mine has a problem with anger and blows his top at the slightest provocation. This upsets everyone around him, and he feels guilty about his outburst afterwards. Fortunately, he is improving, as I've encouraged him to take ten slow, deep breaths before reacting. I then suggest he visualize the outcome he most desires from the situation. The results are amazing, when he pauses long enough to do it.

Upsetting though it can be, my relative's ability to immediately vent his anger is healthier than the approach used by many other people. They repress their feelings of anger. There are many reasons for this. They may be lacking in confidence, and find it hard to assert themselves. They may have been taught by their parents not to show any emotion whatsoever in public. This problem can be resolved if these people visualize past situations in which they failed to express their emotions, and then relive the experiences, seeing themselves handling the situation in a calm, confident, assertive manner.

Most fears are due to feelings of insecurity and a basic lack of confidence. These can all be overcome with visualizations that show you acting in a confident, positive manner.

Guilt is a particularly crippling emotion. In actuality, it is a good emotion, as it prevents us from doing things that we know are wrong. However, many people carry feelings of guilt for years, and this holds them back, as they do not feel good about themselves. Of course, the best remedy is to apologize, and to rectify your mistake. However, this is not always possible. Realize that everyone makes numerous mistakes along the way. Visualize the scenes that caused the guilt. Express your sorrow. Repeat the scene, but this time visualize it on a small screen. Again express your regrets. Finally, visualize the scene again on an even smaller screen.

Express your regrets, and say that you have learned from the experience and will endeavor to do better in the future. Allow the small screen to get smaller and smaller until it disappears.

Frequently, the guilt that people harbor should not be there anyway. If you have to turn down a request from someone else, for instance, you might feel guilty about it, even if your reasons for saying "no" were legitimate. An acquaintance of mine felt guilty when he failed to stop and help the victims of a traffic accident. He didn't stop because two of the victims were fighting each other. However, he used his cell phone to call for help. I think he did everything necessary in that particular situation, and had nothing to feel guilty about.

Of course, the emotion of guilt is still present, regardless of whether or not it was deserved. The remedy is to visualize the entire incident, and tell yourself that you did all that you were capable of doing at that particular moment. Pause, and wait for your body to respond. If you feel a positive response, or no response at all, say goodbye to the incident and let it go. If your body reacts negatively, repeat the visualization again and again until your body signals that you can let it go.

Suggested affirmations include, "I enjoy being in control of my emotions" and "I am a positive person and have no time for negative thoughts or emotions."

Eliminating Painful Memories

It would be hard to go through life without being hurt by others. Sometimes others can hurt us intentionally, but often we make matters worse inside our heads. Fortunately, the pain that these hurts create can be eliminated using creative visualization.

Relax, and then go to your secret room. Visualize yourself relaxing in your special, secret room. In your imagination, you hear a knock on the door. You open it and invite your guest in. Your guest is a nurse. She is a special nurse who takes away painful thoughts, feelings, and memories.

You sit down again and allow the nurse to feel your pulse. She stands in front of you and rests both hands on your shoulders. Her hands are warm, and you can feel the pleasant, gentle heat spreading throughout your body. At the same time it feels as if she is drawing all of the painful memories out of your body. You experience a sense of release and happiness that you have not felt in a long time. Once she has drawn all of the hurt out of your body, she smiles, rubs her hands briskly, and asks you to call on her whenever you need her assistance. She sees herself out, while you relax for as long as you wish. When you feel ready, return to everyday life. You will discover your painful memories have disappeared, and you will feel full of happiness and contentment.

Repeat this visualization as often as necessary until all of the pain has completely disappeared.

Suggested affirmations include, "I let go of the past" and "I enjoy thinking positive and productive thoughts."

Improving Your Relationships

Creative visualization can increase the pleasure and happiness you enjoy in a close relationship. Naturally, you should keep the love and magic alive in as many different ways as possible. You should also work on building a successful life together, while maintaining your own personal identity. Realize that neither you nor your partner are perfect, and that you both will make mistakes. However, with love on both sides, your relationship can build and grow throughout a lifetime.

In your visualization sessions, picture your partner and yourself enjoying happy, fun times together. If you are going through a difficult time in your relationship, visualize a successful outcome. Visualize the two of you communicating effectively and openly, no matter what is occurring in your lives.

Suggested affirmations include, "I am understanding and considerate of (partner's name) at all times," "I love sharing my life with (partner's name)," and "I keep finding more ways to enjoy my relationship with (partner's name)."

Managing Time

Most people complain about lack of time. However, we all have exactly the same amount of time every day. Some people achieve much more in their allotted 24 hours than others, but it is possible to improve your time-management skills with creative visualization. If you find yourself totally overburdened with work, you should consider delegating some of it, or learning some time-management skills. The most useful advice I have ever received on this subject was to make a list of everything that had to be achieved, and to then number them in order of importance. I was to finish the most important task before moving on to the second item on the list, and to gradually work my way down to the bottom. Even if I failed to complete everything on the list, all of the important tasks would be done. The items remaining would be placed on a new list of things to be done on the following day.

Procrastination is another problem. If you keep putting undesirable tasks off indefinitely, sooner or later you'll experience problems. Read the section on motivation for suggestions on how to eliminate this difficulty.

In your creative visualization sessions, see yourself doing everything that you have to do, without stress or worry. Visualize yourself completing the most important tasks first, and having breaks every now and again to relax. See yourself meeting deadlines by being efficient and well organized.

Suggested affirmations include, "I make excellent use of my time" and "Every day I achieve what I set out to accomplish."

Improving Memory

Strange as it may sound, you have a perfect memory. Everything you have ever experienced is stored in your brain.

The only problem is that your recall is sometimes faulty. Fortunately, this can be helped with creative visualization.

Whenever you find yourself struggling to remember a fact or someone's name, relax and visualize the information coming to you. You might like to visualize your brain as a huge computer. When you ask it for information, the printer immediately starts and the information is delivered to you. You might like to picture yourself sitting in front of a computer, typing a question. You wait for a moment or two, until the answer appears on the screen. I prefer to visualize a sheet of paper emerging from my mind and floating in front of me, with all the information I require printed on it.

The important thing is not to panic, especially if you are in an exam or test of some sort. Stay relaxed and request the information you need. If it is in your mind, it will come to you.

Suggested affirmations are, "I remember names and faces clearly" and "I remember everything that is important to me."

Eliminating Fears

Fears and phobias respond particularly well to creative visualization. This is because you can visualize whatever it is that is causing the problem in a safe, even detached, manner. If, for instance, you have a phobia about spiders, you could visualize yourself watching a small spider several yards away from you. Notice the response of your body to that picture and make the spider move farther away, or a little bit closer, depending on the reaction of your body. Over a period of time, you'll be able to allow the spider to come closer and closer, until finally it is resting on your hand, without causing any physical response in your body.

Suppose you had a fear of heights. You could start by visualizing yourself outside a tall building. You go in and walk up one flight of stairs and look out the window. Notice the reaction of your body as you look down at the ground. If your body feels calm and relaxed, walk up another flight of stairs and look down again. Keep on doing this until you reach the top of the building, or your body gives a negative response at any level. If it responds negatively, move away from the window, and take a few deep breaths, saying to yourself, "I'm calm and relaxed." Return to the window and look down again. Keep on doing this until your body ceases to react. Then climb up another flight of stairs and look down again.

Visualizing your concerns in this way gradually defuses and eliminates their effectiveness until finally they cease to be a problem.

Suggested affirmations include, "I am free of past concerns" and "I have faith in my ability to control my thoughts and actions."

Increasing Self-Esteem

Low self-esteem afflicts millions of people, and prevents them from achieving all that they could accomplish. People with healthy levels of self-esteem feel good about themselves, and as a result are more likely to achieve success than people with low self-esteem. There is a strong link between good self-esteem, happiness, and success.

Where does good self-esteem come from? It's a combination of feeling good about yourself and reflecting those beliefs out into the world. It comes from inside you, and is not dependent on the views of others. It's a way of being that is necessary for feelings of contentment, happiness, and personal security. With good self-esteem you can weather temporary setbacks and failures, as you know that they are only temporary and that success is just around the corner. Henry Ford said: "Failure is the opportunity to begin again more intelligently."

Fortunately, creative visualization is an effective way of gaining more self-esteem. In your visualizations see yourself as worthy of the very best that life has to offer. Like, love, respect, and accept yourself. Picture yourself as confident, relaxed, and completely in control in every type of situation. Start by picturing scenes from the past that showed you in a good light. Maybe you were congratulated or honored in some sort of way. Once you have done that, visualize yourself speaking with someone you greatly admire. Listen as this person tells you what he or she most admires about you. You may like to visualize yourself receiving a standing ovation in front of a huge crowd of people. They all admire, respect, and love you. Once you have visualized some positive scenes, deliberately choose situations that you might have found difficult in the past. However, in your visualization, see yourself handling them all in exactly the way you would want. See yourself using positive body language, exuding confidence and happiness. It can be helpful to go through a complete day in your visualization, doing all the things that you normally do, but doing them in the way you want them to be from now on. See yourself maintaining eye contact with others, for instance. See yourself smiling more than ever before, because you are genuinely happy and enjoying your new life.

Accompany this with positive affirmations that reinforce the fact that you are fine exactly the way you are. You might say, "I like people, and people like me. I am outgoing and confident" or "I choose to be all that I can be."

Loving Yourself

We should all love and nurture ourselves. In fact, we should do this constantly. Unfortunately, many people loathe and despise themselves. It is hard to achieve anything when you consider yourself an enemy rather than a friend. Develop some positive affirmations to use whenever you find yourself thinking negative thoughts. You might repeat something like: "I love myself unconditionally."

In your visualization sessions, tell yourself how much you love and appreciate yourself. Be particularly aware of any reactions your body may make to these positive statements. Afterwards you can create affirmations to counteract any negativity revealed by your body.

Smile at yourself whenever you see yourself in a mirror, and express your love for yourself, silently if necessary.

Nurture yourself by giving yourself small pleasures on a regular basis. Whenever you do anything good or worthwhile, silently congratulate yourself and acknowledge that you are a worthwhile, lovable person.

Suggested affirmations include, "I love myself" and "I have many talents and abilities that help make me the wonderful person I am." There is no need to be modest when composing affirmations of this sort.

Motivating Yourself

Nothing happens without motivation. Motivation is generated automatically when you're excited about something and can't wait to get started. However, motivation can sometimes slow down and even disappear once the initial excitement has gone. Fortunately, you can use creative visualization to restore your motivation whenever necessary. Relax, and then visualize the successful accomplishment of your goal. Allow yourself to feel the pleasure and satisfaction you'll have once the task has been completed. Go back to when you first started on the project. Feel the excitement and motivation you had then. Once you have visualized the completion and start of the project, return to the present moment and allow all the enthusiasm, energy, and motivation you have absorbed to carry over into the present. You will open your eyes after the visualization feeling motivated once more. Repeat as often as necessary.

Sometimes you might have to gain motivation to work on a project that holds no interest for you. In this instance, visualize some of your previous successes. It makes no difference what area of your life they occurred in. Allow the feelings of joy and satisfaction of accomplishment to fill every cell of your body. Once you have done that, think of the project you are currently involved in, and experience those same feelings as you look at it. When you feel ready, open your eyes and start on the project. You may have to repeat this visualization several times but it will give you the necessary motivation to complete the task.

Suggested affirmations include, "I enjoy achieving my goals" and "I am successful and on the way to even greater achievements."

Solving Problems

Everyone experiences problems from time to time. Creative visualization allows you to put your problems in perspective, and resolve them smoothly and without stress or undue aggravation.

Next time you have a problem of any sort, sit down and relax in the usual way. Think about one or two pleasant activities that you have enjoyed recently. When you feel ready, think about the problem you are concerned with. Visualize a scene in which this problem occurs. Allow yourself to watch it unfold in a detached manner, as if you were watching it happen to someone else on a television screen. Once you have viewed the entire scene, go back to the start and watch this scene again. However, this time the problem has been resolved and you are watching the scene on a giant cinema screen. Notice the differences between the two scenes. See what needs to be done to correct the problem. If there are other people involved, you may want to look at this scene again from their points of view.

So far, this has not been a normal creative visualization, as we have deliberately left out all emotion. Once you feel that you know everything necessary to resolve the difficulty, play the scene again on a large screen, but this time add color, energy, and emotion. Visualize yourself overcoming the problem without tension or stress.

When you feel ready, open your eyes and carry on with your day, ready and prepared to do your part to resolve the problem in a way that benefits everyone. You may need to repeat this exercise several times before you can experience the final visualization without any negative emotions creeping in.

Suggested affirmations include, "I trust my judgment and have total faith in myself" and "I make good decisions after careful thought and study."

Restoring Your Soul

One of my favorite poets is William Butler Yeats. In his poem *Sailing to Byzantium* he wrote:

An aged man is but a paltry thing,
A tattered coat upon a stick, unless
Soul clap its hands and sing, and louder sing
For every tatter in its mortal dress.

The line "a tattered coat upon a stick" is tragic until you read the next line and learn that the soul claps its hands and sings. This is what you must do at every opportunity. Let your soul clap its hands and sing. It is almost as important to encourage other people's souls to sing, also.

Creative visualizations automatically nurture your soul. Whenever you slow down, pause, and relax, you are feeding your eternal soul. You can also perform visualizations that are intended to restore your soul.

Relax in the usual way, and then allow your mind to be as still as possible. Focus on your breathing, and become aware of the life force that is in every cell of your body. Express your love for yourself. Realize that you are perfect exactly as you are, and that you are here to fulfil some universal purpose. Thank your soul for allowing you to experience this lifetime. Visualize yourself spending time with family and friends and being able to see their eternal souls. Notice the inner beauty that everyone you meet possesses. Send thoughts of love and gratitude to your soul.

Enjoy this special time for as long as you can. When you feel ready, take three deep breaths, open your eyes, stretch, and then carry on with your day. You will notice an immediate change in your energy levels after this visualization. You will also, for a while, become aware of the truth in the saying that we are spiritual beings having a physical experience. Unfortunately, the pressures of everyday life tend to make these feelings short-lived. Consequently, you should nurture your soul in this way as often as you can.

Suggested affirmations include, "I am a valuable, integral part of the universal life force" and "I am fulfilling my cosmic destiny."

Visualizing Your Ideal Life

This is an extremely enjoyable exercise to do. All you need do is relax and think of some happy moments from your past. Relive them as vividly as you can. Feel the emotions you felt, and how happy you were. Continue reliving happy moments from your past for as long as you wish. When you feel ready, project yourself into the future and visualize your life as it will be five years from now. Obviously, world events might change the picture you create, but this does not matter. The picture that you create in your mind will give you a strong sense of what your life is likely to be like. Think about the home you will be living in. You might even choose to live in another city, state, or even country. Visualize yourself as you go through an entire day, from the time you wake up in the morning until you go back to bed at night. Notice everything that is different from the way your life is now.

Once you have done this, ask yourself if this is exactly how you want your life to be in five years' time. If not, go through an entire day again, this time living the life that you want to lead. Feel free to change anything at all that you were not happy with before.

After reliving this perfect day, think about the successes and achievements that you have accomplished during the previous five years. (Of course, although you are looking back at them in your visualization, the entire five years is actually in the future.) See yourself recognized and honored by your peers for your achievements and contributions.

Enjoy this creative visualization for as long as possible. Particularly enjoy the feelings of pride, success, and happiness that you experience as you look at your accomplishments over this five-year period.

When you feel ready, return to the present and open your eyes. Think about the visualization and ask yourself if you are on track to achieving this glorious future. Think about the changes you will have to make in your life if you are to accomplish them. Are you prepared to pay the price to allow this future to unfold? If not, go through the visualization again creating a more modest future for yourself. See if it feels as satisfying as the first one. Chances are, it won't. Remember that you can achieve anything you set your mind on. How could you enjoy a perfect future if you settled for something less than what your innermost desires tell you?

Think about the perfect life you visualized. It doesn't have to come into being all at once. Divide it up into small steps. Visualize yourself achieving each one in turn, and make it happen.

Suggested affirmations include, "Today is a fabulous day for me" and "I am happy, healthy, successful and in control of my life."

CHAPTER SIXTEEN

WHEN IT DOESN'T WORK

"As he thinketh in his heart, so is he."

—PROVERBS 23:7

In a perfect world everything would go according to plan, and there'd be no delays, frustrations, or hold-ups. The world would be rather boring if everything worked like that, but all the same, it can be highly frustrating to put time and effort into a task and not receive the expected results.

There are a number of factors that might be preventing you from reaping the rewards of creative visualization.

Your visualization sessions should be something that you look forward to. They should be effortless and enjoyable. Once you are used to the process, you should be able to relax quickly and easily. If you find it hard to relax, or find yourself preoccupied with other concerns, it is better to abandon the session and try again when you feel less stressed.

Your visualizations should be performed in a playful, cheerful manner. This eliminates any possibility of negative thoughts interfering with your visualization. It also enables you to relax more easily. It is hard to relax and focus when you are grimly determined. Do not attempt to force an outcome. Have fun with your visualizations.

Do you know exactly what you want? Many people know what they don't want, but have no clear picture of what they do want. It is vital for successful visualization that you know exactly what it is that you want, and that you focus on that particular desire until it becomes real. If you keep changing your mind about what you want, you will have difficulty in manifesting anything.

You should also visualize what you want, but not concern yourself with how it occurs. You will experience difficulty if you insist that it manifest itself in a certain way or through a specific series of actions.

If your visualization is totally unrelated to anything you have thought in the past, your mind is likely to resist every effort you make. After all, it's happy with you the way you are now, and does not want to change anything. Consequently, you may continue to wallow in negative thoughts and forget to think positively or to repeat your affirmations. In this example, success would be impossible until you trained your mind to accept the new ways of thinking.

Another possibility is that on a subconscious level you don't believe you can attain the goal you are visualizing. This might relate to self-esteem issues or a lack of faith in your abilities. The remedy for this is to use affirmations as well as the visualizations.

If you are visualizing health, love, and prosperity while these things are absent in your life, you might feel guilty about even thinking of the possibility. This negativity will also prevent you from reaching your goal.

Another possibility is that although you would like to have whatever it is you are visualizing, you are not passionate about it. You are unlikely to achieve your goal unless you feel excited about achieving it.

Your desire has to become real in your mind. It will not manifest itself until you can feel, touch, taste, smell, and savour your desire all the time. Your desire needs to be constantly in your mind, not always at a conscious level, magnetizing the universe and drawing to you whatever it happens to be.

You need to be determined. Many people are half-hearted in their visualizations. You cannot expect great things to happen if you spend five or ten minutes a day visualizing something, and then forget about it until it is time to do your visualizations again on the next day.

You also need to help the universe manifest your goals. Most goals require hard work and effort as well as visualization. You can visualize for hours a day, but if you're not going to raise a finger to help it become a reality, your desire is likely to remain simply a dream.

Researchers at Emory University in Atlanta, Georgia, performed an interesting experiment that demonstrates the benefits of working toward a goal. They formed two groups of volunteers. The first group played a simple computer game, and were financially rewarded each time they were successful. The people in the second group were rewarded without having to do anything to earn it. The researchers measured brain activity in the striatum, which is the part of the brain responsible for reward-processing and pleasure, and discovered that the volunteers who earned their rewards received more stimulation in their brains. Greg Berns, Associate Professor of Psychiatry and Behavioral Science at the university, said, "When you do things for your reward, it's clearly more important to the brain. The subjects were more aroused when they had to do something to get the money relative to when they passively received the money."[1]

You also need persistence. A major reason for failure in creative visualization is discouragement. If you strongly desire the outcome you are visualizing, you need to keep on with your visualizations, no matter how long it takes. Everyone wants immediate success. However, this does not occur all, or even much, of the time. You need to keep working at it until it becomes a reality. Obviously, if you give up, the desired result will not occur. As you know, your mind can play tricks on you. Sometimes your subconscious mind will be working on major changes, while your conscious mind is telling you that you are wasting your time.

You may have set a time span for your visualization, and become disappointed when it didn't manifest within that time. The spiritual world lives in the eternal now and does not recognize time. Rest assured that if you continually visualize your desire, it will manifest when it is ready.

Another problem occurs surprisingly often. You must keep your visualizations to yourself. When you talk to other people about your visualizations they become less effective. Your ego and the opinions of others enter the equation, and weaken them. Talk about the process of visualization, by all means, but keep the particular desires that you are manifesting to yourself.

Whatever the problem may be, don't stop visualizing. You might be closer to success than you think. All creative visualizations take time to manifest in your life, and you need to allow as much time as necessary for this to happen. Even visualizing a parking space or a small line at the bank takes a certain amount of time. Visualizing a new car or a house will obviously take much longer. Be patient, no matter what it is you are visualizing.

You might find it helpful to visualize your goal more frequently. Many people visualize in a half-hearted manner. If you visualize once or twice and then give up, you are unlikely to achieve your goals. However, if you visualize a successful outcome twice every single day, and also think about your desire whenever you have a spare moment, success will inevitably follow.

Even when you are not visualizing, think about your goals as often as possible. Enjoy daydreaming about the beneficial changes in your life that will come as a result. Contrary to what most people think, daydreaming is not a waste of time, especially if it is directed toward a goal. The more you daydream about it, the greater the desire for it. You will start looking forward to the achievement with a sense of excitement and anticipation.

You might find it helpful to add more emotion to your visualizations. Emotion wins over logic every time. You might desire something logically, but it is unlikely to become a reality unless you stir in a liberal amount of emotion. Thoughts without emotion flit through our minds all the time. They possess no power or energy. It is essential that you include as much emotion as possible into your visualizations.

One of my students found it hard to add emotion to her goals. She felt that it was her emotions that always let her down, and consequently she would fare better in life by experiencing them as seldom as possible. I felt this was a rather strange way of getting through life, but she had suffered a great deal, and this was her way of handling any potential difficulties. I suggested that, after the relaxation stage, she should daydream about her goal. She should also think about other happy and positive moments in her life, trying to recapture everything she experienced at those times. Only after doing this, and reliving the feelings and emotions that these positive experiences provided, should she carry on with her visualization.

Boredom is the final obstacle to success. This is a surprising problem, as your desires should be so exciting and motivating that boredom would be the last thing on your mind. However, it can happen. The remedy to this is to make your visualizations so vivid and stimulating that boredom totally disappears. You might like to change the images you think about, for the sake of variety. You should definitely add more emotion and feeling to your visualization. You should also question whether or not you really desire whatever it is you are visualizing.

You should act as if you already possess whatever it is you are visualizing. If you are visualizing health, for instance, live each day as if you already possess perfect health. If you are a salesperson and are visualizing becoming a sales manager, act as if you already have the job. You will act and carry yourself differently as a result, and this will help you achieve your goal. If you are visualizing wealth, immediately start feeling abundant and look around for opportunities to progress financially. Become more generous, too. Strange as it may seem, increased generosity will help you reach your goal more quickly.

Action Exercise

Visualizing on its own is not always enough. Sooner or later you need to act. This necessity paralyzes some people into inaction. Fear, doubt, and worry are created when you focus on what you don't want rather than what you do. Fortunately, it is a simple matter to determine when to act. All you need do is think quietly about your goal and notice what responses are created in your mind and body. If your thought creates fear, anxiety, or any other negative reaction, it is not the right time to act. Examine your thoughts and feelings to determine what is behind these negative responses. You may need to work on these problems before continuing. Repeat this experiment on a regular basis. Only when you receive a positive response from your mind and body should you act. At this point, your actions will seem effortless and you will progress quickly.

CHAPTER SEVENTEEN

IT'S UP TO YOU

"Few moments are more pleasing than those in which the mind is concerting measures for a new undertaking."

—SAMUEL JOHNSON

I have heard many amazing stories about people who have visualized something and then had it manifest in their own lives.

One was a man I worked with many years ago. He worked as a salesman for a printing machinery company. He was an expert at solving problems that occurred to the binding and folding machinery that is used in the printing trade. His dream was to own a print finishing business.

However, it seemed totally impossible. He had a young family, a large mortgage, and no business skills. However, he began visualizing himself running his own business. He visualized the exact premises he desired, the specific machines he wanted to have, and a number of regular, good-paying customers. Eighteen months after he started visualizing this dream, one of his customers asked if he would be interested in buying into his business. My friend did not need to put any money into the venture, and was able to buy his half share over a period of time from the work and expertise he provided. His visualization paid off.

Joanna, a student of mine, was a thirty-five-year-old mother, bringing up two children on her own. She had always been slightly overweight, but when her marriage ended she began eating for comfort. In two years she gained seventy-five pounds. After trying numerous diets with no success, Joanna began visualizing herself at the weight she wanted to be. It took twelve months, but now Joanna looks better, and feels better, than ever. She also feels more attractive and has started dating again.

A young man working in a publishing company dreamed of making his living as a writer. It was not until after he began visualizing himself as a full-time writer that his dreams became a reality. I was that young man.

Carol Burnett, the famous actress, is an excellent example of the power of visualization. She had a poverty-stricken childhood, and was brought up by her grand-mother. Carol had an impossible dream. She wanted to go to UCLA, and she knew in her heart that she would get there. "I never thought about the possibility of not going," she recalled. "I would imagine myself taking the classes, being on the campus, learning everything I wanted to learn. Every day I would think about it. Even though there didn't seem any way I could go, I knew I would." One day, while in her final year at high school, she went to the mailbox and found an envelope addressed to her. In it was the exact amount of money needed to pay for her first year's tuition. Carol said, "I still, to this day, don't know who sent it."[1]

Obviously, it is unlikely that some anonymous benefactor will send you money through the post. However, you can expect incredible things to happen. Once you start visualizing on a regular basis, for whatever it is you want, the universe will start working on your behalf, and you will be amazed at the number of opportunities that will open up for you.

Don't short-change yourself. Your dreams can come true. Visualize yourself already in possession of your goal. Keep that picture constantly in your mind as you work toward making it a reality.

If you are not in control of your destiny, seize control now and use the techniques in this book to help you achieve your full potential. The happiest people in the world are those who know what they want to achieve, and are steadily working toward their goals.

Success is not an accident. Creative visualization will enable you to transform your life and make your dreams come true.

SUGGESTED READING

Achterberg, Jeanne. *Imagery in Healing: Shamanism and Modern Medicine*. Boston: Shambala Publications, Inc., 1985.

Arnheim, Rudolf. *Visual Thinking*. Berkeley: University of California Press, 1972.

Assagioli, Roberto. *Psychosynthesis*. New York: Hobbs, Dorman and Co., Inc., 1965.

Bacci, Ingrid. *The Art of Effortless Living*. New York: Vision Works, 2000.

Backley, Steve, with Ian Stafford. *The Winning Mind: A Guide to Achieving Success and Overcoming Failure*. London: Aurum Press Limited, 1996.

Behrend, Genevieve. *Your Invisible Power*. Marina del Rey: DeVorss and Company, 1951.

Suggested Reading

Bry, Adelaide. *Visualization: Directing the Movies of Your Mind*. New York: Barnes and Noble, Inc., 1978.

Capacchione, Lucia. *Visioning: Ten Steps to Designing the Life of Your Dreams*. New York: Jeremy P. Tarcher/Putnam, 2000.

Cornell, Ann Weiser. *The Power of Focusing: A Practical Guide to Emotional Self-Healing*. New York: MJF Books, 1996.

Coué, Emil. *Self-Mastery Through Conscious AutoSuggestion*. London: Allen and Unwin Limited, 1922.

Denning, Melita and Osborne Phillips. *Creative Visualization for the Fulfillment of Your Desires*. St. Paul: Llewellyn Publications, 1980.

Dyer, Wayne. *Manifest Your Destiny: The Nine Spiritual Principles for Getting Everything You Want*. New York: HarperCollins, 1997.

Fanning, Patrick. *Visualization for Change*. Oakland: New Harbinger Publications, Inc., 1988.

Fries, Jan. *Visual Magick*. Oxford, UK: Mandrake of Oxford, 1992.

Gallwey, W. Timothy. *The Inner Game of Tennis*. New York: Random House, Inc., 1974.

Gallwey, W. Timothy. *The Inner Game of Golf*. New York: Random House, Inc., 1981.

Garfield, P. *Creative Dreaming*. New York: Simon and Schuster, Inc., 1975.

Gawain, Shakti. *Creative Visualization*. San Rafael: CA, New World Library, 1978.

Gendlin, Eugene T. *Focusing*. New York: Everest House, 1978.

Gladwell, Malcolm. *Blink: The Power of Thinking Without Thinking*. New York: Little, Brown and Company, 2005.

Glouberman, Dina. *Life Choices and Life Changes Through Imagework: The Art of Developing Personal Vision*. London: Unwin Hyman Ltd., 1989.

Heads, Ian, and Geoff Armstrong (editors). *Winning Attitudes: Sport's Messages for Achievements in Life*. South Yarra, Australia: Hardie Grant Books, 2000.

Suggested Reading

Holmes, Paul. *The Inner World Outside: Object Relations Theory and Psychodrama*. London: Routledge, 1992.

Kehoe, John. *Mind Power Into the 21st Century*. West Vancouver, Canada: Zoetic Inc., 1996.

Maltz, Maxwell. *The Magic Power of Self-Image Psychology*. Englewood Cliffs, NJ: Prentice-Hall, Inc., 1964.

Maltz, Maxwell. *Psycho-Cybernetics*. New York: Pocket Books, 1966.

Markham, Ursula. *Life Scripts: How to Talk to Yourself for Positive Results*. Shaftesbury, UK: Element Books Limited, 1993.

Martens, Rainer. *Coaches Guide to Sport Psychology*. Champaign, IL: Human Kinetics Publishers, Inc., 1987.

Masters, Robert, and Jean Houston. *Mind Games*. New York: Dell Books, Inc., 1972.

McKim, Robert. *Experiences in Visual Thinking*. Monterey: Brooks Cole Publishing Co., 1972.

Millman, Dan. *The Warrior Athlete: Body, Mind and Spirit*. Walpole, NH: Stillpoint Publishing, 1979.

Myss, Caroline. *Why People Don't Heal and How They Can*. New York: Harmony Books, 1997.

Orlick, Terry. *In Pursuit of Excellence: How to Win in Sport and Life Through Mental Training*. Champaign, IL: Leisure Press, 1990.

Osborn, A. F. *Applied Imagination: Principles and Procedures of Creative Problem Solving*. New York: Charles Scribner's Sons, Inc., 1963.

Peale, Norman Vincent. *The Power of Positive Thinking*. Tadworth, UK: The World's Work (1913) Limited, 1953.

Porter, Kay, and Judy Foster. *The Mental Athlete*. New York: Ballantine Books, 1987.

Richardson, A. *Mental Imagery*. New York: Springer Publishing Co., 1969.

Robertson, Ian. *The Mind's Eye: An Essential Guide to Boosting Your Mental Power*. London: Bantam Press, 2002.

Rossman, Martin L. *Healing Yourself: A Step By Step Process for Better Health Through Imagery*. New York: Walker and Co., 1987.

Samuels, Mike, and Samuels, Nancy. *Seeing With the Mind's Eye: The History, Techniques and Uses of Visualization*. New York: Random House, Inc., 1975.

Segal, S. J. *The Adaptive Functions of Imagery*. New York: Academic Press, 1971.

Shinn, Florence Scovel. *The Game of Life and How to Play It*. London: L. N. Fowler and Company Limited, 1925.

Siegel, Bernie. *Peace, Love and Healing*. London: Rider and Company, 1990.

Simonton, O. C., S. Matthews-Simonton, and J. L. Creighton, *Getting Well Again*. New York: Bantam Books, 1980.

Tutko, Thomas, and Umberto Tosi. *Sports Psyching*. Los Angeles: Westwood Publishing, 1976.

Ventrella, Scott W. *The Power of Positive Thinking in Business*. New York: The Free Press, 2001.

Waitley, Denis. *The New Dynamics of Goal Setting: Flextactics for a Fast-Changing World*. New York: William Morrow and Company, Inc., 1996.

NOTES

Introduction

1. Norman Vincent Peale, *The Power of Positive Thinking* (Tadworth, UK: The World's Work (1913) Limited, 1953), 225–229.

2. The Imagineers, *Walt Disney Imagineering: A Behind the Dreams Look at Making the Magic Real* (New York: Disney Enterprises, Inc., 1996).

Chapter One

1. Arnold Schwarzenegger, quoted in John Kehoe, *Mind Power Into the 21st Century* (West Vancouver, Canada: Zoetic Inc., 1996), 13–14.

2. Steven Starker, *Fantastic Thought: All About Dreams, Daydreams, Hallucinations, and Hypnosis* (Englewood Cliffs, NJ: Prentice-Hall, Inc., 1982), 21.

3. R. Holt, "Imagery: The Return of the Ostracized." Article in *American Psychologist* 19, 1964, 254–264.

4. Albert Einstein, quoted in Ian Robertson, *The Mind's Eye: An Essential Guide to Bosting Your Mental Power.* (London, UK: Bantam Press, 2002), 90.

5. Earl Nightingale, *This is Earl Nightingale* (Garden City, NY: Doubleday and Company, 1969), 291.

6. Michael Mayell, quoted in "Wisdom on the Wire" by Monique Devereux. Article in *Canvas, Weekend Herald*, Auckland, NZ, 17–18 April, 2004.

Chapter Two

1. A. R. Luria, *The Mind of a Mnemonist: A Little Book About a Vast Memory* (New York: Basic Books, Inc., 1968), 84.

2. David Marks, "Imagery and Consciousness: A Theoretical Review from an Individual Perspective." Article in *Journal of Mental Imagery*, 2, 1977, 285–347.

3. R. M. Suinn (editor), *Psychology in Sports: Methods and Applications* (Minneapolis: Burgess International Group, 1980), 83. Professor Suinn is a former member of the U.S. Olympic Committee, Sport Psychology Committee and team psychologist for U.S. summer and winter men's and women's Olympic Teams. He is also the past president of the American Psychological Association.

Chapter Three

1. Robert J. Sternberg, James C. Kaufman, and Jean E. Pretz, *The Creativity Conundrum: A Propulsion Model of Kinds of Creative Contributions* (New York: Psychology Press, 2002), 188.

Chapter Four

1. Denis Waitley and Reni L. Witt, *The Joy of Working* (New York, NY: Ballantine Books, Inc., 1986), 252.

Chapter Seven

1. Roberto Assagioli, *Psychosynthesis* (New York: The Viking Press, Inc., 1971. Originally published by Hobbs, Dorman and Co., Inc., 1965), 146–147.

Chapter Eight

1. There are many books available on the causes of psychosomatic illnesses. The classic book on the subject is *Psychosomatic Medicine* by Franz Alexander, MD (New York: W. W. Norton Company, 1950).

2. Florence Scovel Shinn, *The Game of Life and How to Play It* (London: I. N. Fowler and Company Limited, 1925), 51.

3. Scott W. Ventrella, *The Power of Positive Thinking in Business* (New York: The Free Press, 2001), 102.

4. Norman Vincent Peale, *The Power of Positive Thinking*, 9–10.

Chapter Eleven

1. Terry Orlick, *In Pursuit of Excellence: How to Win in Sport and Life Through Mental Training* (Champaign, IL: Leisure Press, 1990), 71.

2. Ian Robertson, *The Mind's Eye: An Essential Guide to Boosting Your Mental Power* (London, UK: Bantam Press, 2002), 196.

3. Jack Nicklaus, quoted in Harry Mills, *The Mental Edge: Unlocking the Secrets of Inner Selling* (Lower Hutt, NZ: Mills Publications, 1994), 101.

4. Jack Nicklaus, quoted in Rainer Martens, *Coaches Guide to Sport Psychology* (Champaign, IL: Human Kinetics Publishers, Inc., 1987), 77.

5. Arnold Haultain, *The Mystery of Golf* (Boston, MA: Houghton Mifflin Company, 1908). Other books that discuss the mind game of golf include *The Inner Game of Golf* by W. Timothy Gallwey (New York: Random House, Inc., 1981), *Holographic Golf* by Larry Miller (New York: HarperCollins, Inc., 1993), *Exploring the Zone* by Larry Miller (Gretna, LA: Pelican Publishing Co., Inc., 2001), *Mental Management for Great Golf* by Dr. Bee Epstein-Shepherd (New York: McGraw-Hill, Inc., 1996), and *Think Like Tiger* by John Andrisani (New York: G. P. Putnam's Sons, 2002).

6. Mark McGwire, quoted in Scott W. Ventrella, *The Power of Positive Thinking in Business* (New York: The Free Press, 2001), 60.

7. Danni Roche, quoted in *Winning Attitudes: Sport's Messages for Achievements in Life*, edited by Ian Heads and Geoff Armstrong (South Yarra, Australia: Hardie Grant Books in association with the Australian Olympic Committee, 2000), 113–114.

8. Herb Elliott, Introduction to *Winning Attitudes*, 11–12.

9. Brian Orser, quoted in Terry Orlick, *In Pursuit of Excellence: How to Win in Sport and Life Through Mental Training* (Champaign, IL: Leisure Press, 1990), 68.

10. Craig Karges, *Ignite Your Intuition* (Deerfield, FL: Health Communications, Inc., 1999), 66

11. C. Deschaumes et al, "Relationship Between Mental Imagery and Sporting Performance." Article in *Behavioural Brain Research 45*, 1991, 29–36.

12. Edmund Jacobson, *How to Relax and Have Your Baby* (New York: McGraw-Hill Book Co., Inc., 1965), 110. Edmund Jacobson also wrote *Progressive Relaxation* (Chicago: University of Chicago Press, 1938).

13. Alan Richardson, *Mental Imagery* (London: Routledge and Kegan Paul Limited, 1969).

Chapter Twelve

1. *Wall Street Journal* article, quoted in Scott W. Ventrella, *The Power of Positive Thinking in Business* (New York: The Free Press, 2001), 57.

2. Peter F. Drucker, quoted in "Leadership in Living Organizations" by Peter Senge. Article in *Leading Beyond the Walls*, edited by Marshall Goldsmith (New York: Jossey Bass, Inc., 1999), 76.

Chapter Thirteen

1. Mike Samuels and Nancy Samuels, *Seeing With the Mind's Eye: The History, Techniques and Uses of Visualization* (New York: Random House/Bookworks, 1975), 30.

2. Edmund Jacobson, *Progressive Relaxation* (Chicago, IL: University of Chicago Press, 1929).

3. M. Cutler, *The Nature of the Cancer Process in Relation to a Possible Psychosomatic Influence*. Article in *The Psychological Variables in Human Cancer* (City University of California Press, 1954), 1–16.

4. Bernie Siegel, *Peace, Love and Healing* (London: Rider and Company, 1990), 111.

5. Garrett Porter and Patricia Norris, *Why Me? Learning to Harness the Healing Power of the Human Spirit* (Walpole, NH: Stillpoint Publishing, 1985).

6. Jean Houston, *The Possible Human* (New York: Jeremy B. Tarcher, Inc., 1982), 37.

7. Larry and Valere Althouse, *What You Need Is What You've Got* (York Beach, ME: Samuel Weiser, Inc., 1989), 117–118.

8. Caroline Myss, PhD, *Why People Don't Heal and How They Can* (New York: Harmony Books, 1997), 148.

9. Thomas Holmes, quoted in *Stress: Can We Cope?* Article in *Time*, June 6, 1983, 49.

Chapter Fifteen

1. Steve Backley with Ian Stafford, *The Winning Mind: A Guide to Achieving Success and Overcoming Failure* (London: Aurum Press, 1996), 60.

2. Edwin Hughes, "Musical Memory in Piano Playing and Piano Study," Article in *The Musical Quarterly*, Vol 1, 1915, 592–603.

3. Denis Waitley, *The New Dynamics of Goal Setting: Flextactics for a Fast-Changing World* (New York: William Morrow and Company, Inc., 1996), 54.

4. Henry Moore, quoted in B. Ghiselin, *The Creative Process* (New York: New American Library, 1952), 74.

5. A. F. Osborn, *Applied Imagination: Principles and Procedures of Creative Problem Solving* (New York: Charles Scribner's Sons, 1963).

6. Pablo Picasso, quoted in *The Mystery of Picasso*, a film by Henri-Georges Clouzot, 1956.

7. S. Palmer and M. Neenan, "Double Imagery Procedure." Article in *The Rational Emotive Behaviour Therapist*, 6 (1998), 89–92.

Chapter Sixteen

1. Greg Berns, quoted in *Brain Tests Point to Pleasures of Work*, unattributed Associated Press article published in *The New Zealand Herald*, May 17, 2004, A13.

Chapter Seventeen

1. Carol Burnett, quoted in John Kehoe, *Mind Power Into the 21st Century*, 18–19.

INDEX

Adams, Scott, 81–82

Addictions, 94

Affirmations, 70, 77–92, 95, 97, 108, 113–114, 126, 165–166, 168, 170, 172–175, 178–183, 185, 187–190, 192–195, 197–198, 201

Althouse, Valere, 141

Angel, guardian, 153 155, 179–180

Aquinas, St. Thomas, 4

Aristotle, 4

Assagioli, Roberto, 72–73

Aura, 161

Backley, Steve, 165

Bannister, Roger, 28

Belief, xi, 21–22, 25–36, 66, 78, 80, 84, 139, 158

Berns, Greg, 202

Body test, 32

Boredom, 74–75, 205

Burnett, Carol, 208

Index

Change, 2, 4, 8, 19–20, 23, 26, 29–30, 34, 47, 51, 60, 63–64, 74–75, 78, 80, 85–86, 90, 92–93, 96–98, 106, 157, 164, 171, 173–174, 179, 181–182, 196–197, 205
Cigarette, 180–182
Cobain, Kurt, 47
Columbus, Christopher, 32
Confidence, 20, 28, 57, 81, 93–94, 99, 101, 103–108, 111, 113, 115, 124, 131, 145, 184, 192
Coué, Emile, 79
Creativity, 167

Davison, Michelle, 118
Daydreams, 20–21, 68, 70
Desire, xi, xvi, 2, 5, 11, 15, 20–23, 30, 33, 36–43, 47, 53–56, 58–60, 64, 67–69, 78–81, 85–86, 88–91, 99, 101, 109, 116, 128, 130–131, 149, 157–159, 164, 168, 175, 179, 181–182, 200–205
Disney, Walt, 2
Disneyland, 2
Dykman, Janet, 118

Einstein, Albert, 6, 17
Elliott, Herb, 119
Emory University, 202
Emotions, 124, 178, 183–185, 195, 197, 204–205

Fears, irrational, 177

Gambling, 97
Gould, Glenn, 166
Guided visualization, 99, 108, 151
Guideposts, xiv, xv
Guilt, 183–185

Haultain, Arnold, 119
Health, 0, 2, 7, 22, 34, 57, 78, 80, 82–83, 137–147, 178, 182, 201, 205
Hermes, 137
Hobbes, Thomas, 4
Holmes, Thomas, 142
Holt, Robert, 4
Houston, Jean, 141
Hughes, Edwin, 166

Imagination, 5–6, 17–18, 20–22, 45, 50, 67, 73, 96, 124, 134–135, 139, 141, 146, 167, 177, 186
Insomnia, 145, 182

Jacobson, Edmund, 121
Jesus, 32, 38, 47, 69
Jordan, Michael, 118

Kerrigan, Nancy, 118
Killy, Jean-Claude, 118

Law of manifestation, 23
Lewis, Carl, 120
Lombardi, Vince, 41
Louganis, Greg, 120
Luria, A. R., 17–18

Magic, 10, 21, 43, 70, 149–161, 187
Magnus, Albertus, 4
Marks, David, 18
Marsden, Karen, 119
Mayell, Michael, 7
McGwire, Mark, 119
Meditation, 21, 150
Memory, 57, 109, 188
Monroe, Marilyn, 47
Moore, Henry, 167
Motivation, 4, 73, 111, 188, 193–194
Myss, Caroline, 142

Nesmeth, James, 122–123
Nicklaus, Jack, 118
Nicotine, 65, 180–181
Nightingale, Earl, 6–7
Norris, Pat, 140

Obesity, 178
Olness, Karen, 139
Orlick, Terry, 117
Orser, Brian, 120

Osborn, Alex, 167
Outward Bound School, xii

Passion, 38, 42, 61
Pathworking, 21, 151, 153, 155
Peale, Norman Vincent, 83
Persistence, 202
Pestalozzi, Johann, 6
Porter, Garrett, 140
Prayer, 142
Psychosynthesis, 72

Relaxation, 11–13, 33, 48, 71, 99–103, 107, 121, 182, 204
Richardson, Alan, 121
Roche, Danni, 119

Schwarzenegger, Arnold, 1–2
Secret room, 71, 115, 132, 153–154, 183, 186
Self-esteem, 54–55, 84, 93–95, 107, 111, 145, 190–191, 201
Shamans, 138
Shinn, Florence Scovel, 80
Silent affirmations, 88–89
Simonton, Carl, 138–139
Soul, 48, 132, 138, 195–196
Stress, 7, 20, 45, 48, 120, 124, 132, 138, 144–146, 188, 194–195
Suinn, Richard, 19
Symbols, 19, 140, 156–158

Tarot, 159–160
Tattva, 156–158

Vance, Mike, 2

Waitley, Denis, 41
Wilson, Woodrow, x–xi
Witt, Reni L., 41
Woods, Tiger, 118

Yeats, William Butler, 195